D1566433

# The new offshoring of jobs
# and global development

# The New offshoring of jobs and global development

By Gary Gereffi

ILO Social Policy Lectures
Jamaica, December 2005

*HD*
*2365*
*.G474*
*2006*

Published by the International Institute for Labour Studies

The International Institute for Labour Studies (IILS) was established in 1960 as an autonomous facility within the International Labour Organization (ILO), to further policy research, public debate and the sharing of knowledge on emerging labour and social issues of concern to the ILO and its constituents-labour, business and government.

ISBN 92-9014-805-5 and 978-92-9014-805-0 (Print)
ISBN 92-9014-806-3 and 978-92-9014-806-7 (web pdf)
First published 2006

Copies can ordered from: ILO Publications, International Labour Office, CH-1211 Geneva 22 (Switzerland). For on-line orders, see: www.ilo.org/publns

Photocomposed in Switzerland                                                        BRI
Printed by the International Labour Office, Geneva, Switzerland

# Contents

**Preface** . . . . . . . . . . . . . . . . . . . . . . . . . . . . . . . . . . . . . . . **vii**

**Lecture 1.** **An overview of the contemporary global labour market** . . . . . . . . . . . . . . **1**

The great global job shift . . . . . . . . . . . . . . 1

Offshore outsourcing and development:
Old and new trends . . . . . . . . . . . . . . . . . . . 4

Jobs in the global economy:
A global value chains perspective . . . . . . . . . 5

The contemporary global labour market:
A changing landscape . . . . . . . . . . . . . . . . . 8

Assembly jobs in the global economy . . . . . 10

Full-package production jobs and
buyer-oriented upgrading . . . . . . . . . . . . . 11

Advanced production jobs:
Supplier-oriented upgrading
and industry co-evolution . . . . . . . . . . . . . 13

Knowledge-intensive jobs
in offshore services . . . . . . . . . . . . . . . . . 15

**Lecture 2.** **Global consolidation and industrial upgrading: The promise and perils of development** . . . . . . . . . . . . . . . . . . **17**

Introduction . . . . . . . . . . . . . . . . . . . . . . . 17

v

Global consolidation: China, India
and the apparel industry . . . . . . . . . . . . . . 18

    China: The "Workshop of the world" . . . . . 18

    India: The offshoring of information
    technology services . . . . . . . . . . . . . . . . 21

    Trade rules and global consolidation
    in apparel . . . . . . . . . . . . . . . . . . . . . . 22

Industrial upgrading in Mexico and China
– An international trade perspective . . . . . . . . 26

A note on China's supply chain cities
and industrial upgrading . . . . . . . . . . . . . . 33

Shifting development strategies
and regional linkages . . . . . . . . . . . . . . . . 37

**Lecture 3.** **Globalization and the demand
for governance** . . . . . . . . . . . . . . . . . . . . **39**

(co-authored by Gary Gereffi and Frederick Mayer)

The challenge to globalization . . . . . . . . . . . 39

The nature of market governance . . . . . . . . . 41

Before globalization . . . . . . . . . . . . . . . . . . 43

Globalization and governance deficits . . . . . . . 45

The governance response . . . . . . . . . . . . . . 49

    Social pressures and the demand
    for governance . . . . . . . . . . . . . . . . . . . 50

    Thickening international institutions . . . . . 52

    Strengthening private governance:
    Corporate social responsibility,
    codes of conduct and certification . . . . . . . 53

    Building governance capacity
    in developing countries . . . . . . . . . . . . . 56

Conclusion: Are we at a turning point? . . . . . . 57

References . . . . . . . . . . . . . . . . . . . . . . . . 59

# Preface

The Social Policy Lectures are endowed by the ILO's Nobel Peace Prize of 1969 and dedicated to the memory of David A. Morse, Director-General of the ILO from 1948 to 1970. They are held in major universities of the world with the three-fold aim of stimulating the interest of graduate and post-graduate students in international social policy; of promoting academic work in areas of concern to the ILO; and of encouraging greater dialogue between the academic community on the one hand and policy makers, and business and labour on the other. The International Institute for Labour Studies has been entrusted with the responsibility for organizing the lectures.

The 7th Nobel Peace Prize Social Policy Lectures were hosted by the University of the West Indies, and were held in the Mona Campus of the university in Jamaica during 5-7 December 2005. The lectures were given by Professor Gary Gereffi of Duke University, North Carolina, USA. The central theme of the lectures was "The new offshoring of jobs and global development." Professor Gereffi used the global value chains perspective to look at how offshore outsourcing has affected the quantity and quality of jobs in the global economy. In all there were three lectures, dealing with the following topics: (i) An overview of the contemporary global labour market; (ii) Global consolidation and industrial upgrading: The promise and perils of development; and (iii) Globalization and the demand for governance.

Four main themes run through the lectures. The first is an analytical framework for linking jobs in the industrial structures of both advanced and developing economies through the dynamics of global value chains. The strategies of lead firms - global retailers, branded marketers, and brand-name manufacturers - are reviewed within this framework. A second theme is to conceptualize jobs in the global economy not by their location in particular industries or countries, but by their role in global value chains. Four types of jobs were discussed in this regard: (i) Assembly jobs that involve the processing of imported inputs for exports; (ii) "Full-package" jobs producing finished consumer goods; (iii) Original design manufacturing and own brand manufacturing; and (iv) Knowledge-intensive jobs related to research and development, information technology and business process services. The third theme is that along with the geographical dispersion and fragmentation of production under contemporary globalization, there has been a significant consolidation of global value chains in recent years. These consolidation trends are illustrated with reference to China, India, and the apparel industry. Finally, given the special features of global value chains, the lectures highlight the need for a rethinking of the development agenda in both the developing and advanced industrial economies. In particular, Gereffi argues that there is a need to reconsider the contemporary notions of global corporate social responsibility and private as well as public governance.

The Social Policy Lectures were followed by panel discussions on each lecture. The faculty members and students of the University of the West Indies, staff of the Institute and the ILO social partners in the Caribbean took part in the lectures and discussions. They were concluded with a roundtable meeting that included the ILO tripartite representatives from the Caribbean region - the Government Group, the Caribbean Labour Congress and the Caribbean Employers' Confederation, who reviewed the topics with special reference to the situation in the Caribbean.

The Mona Campus of the University of West Indies was the main venue of the lectures and related events. The entire proceedings of the lectures, panel discussions and roundtable were transmitted via videoconference to the two other major campuses of the University, Cave Hill in Barbados and St. Augustine in Port of Spain. The videoconference facility enabled the academic community of the three campuses to attend the lectures and to take part in interactive discussions on social and labour policy matters. A full-length video recording of the lectures and associated events has been prepared by the university for use by students and researchers and by ILO constituents.

This volume contains the text of the social policy lectures, revised and updated by Gary Gereffi. It is being brought out as a joint publication of the University of the West Indies and the International Institute for Labour Studies. On behalf of the Institute I would like to acknowledge the valuable support and cooperation from Professor Neville Ying and his colleagues at the Mona Business School of the University of West Indies towards organizing the lectures and related events.

I would like to thank Gary Gereffi, a longstanding associate of the International Institute for Labour Studies for having prepared a remarkably elegant set of lectures on a topic on which he has the distinction of being a leading authority. I would also like to thank Professor Frederick Mayer for his help in revising the content of Lecture 3 for publication in this volume. Last but not least, A.V. Jose ably handled the preparation and organization of the event on behalf of the IILS.

Gerry Rodgers
Director
International Institute for Labour Studies

**Gary Gereffi** is Professor of Sociology and Director of the Center on Globalization, Governance and Competitiveness at Duke University, North Carolina, USA. He has published extensively on globalization and development. His major ongoing research projects are: (1) industrial upgrading in East Asia, North America, and Eastern Europe/Central Asia; (2) a book on global consolidation, using a global value chains perspective; and (3) analysing the competitiveness of North Carolina industries in the global economy.

**Frederick Mayer** is Director of Graduate Studies and Associate Professor of Public Policy Studies and Political Science at Duke University's Terry Sanford Institute of Public Policy. His current research focuses on globalization and governance, with particular focus on the labour and environmental impacts of economic integration.

# Lecture 1. An overview of the contemporary global labour market[1]

## The great global job shift

A cover story in the 3 February, 2003 issue of *Business Week* highlighted the impact of global outsourcing over the past several decades on the quality and quantity of jobs in both developed and developing countries (Engardio et al., 2003). The first wave of global outsourcing began in the 1960s and 1970s with the exodus of production jobs in shoes, clothing, cheap electronics, and toys. After that, routine service work, like credit-card receipt processing, airline reservations, and the writing of basic software code began to move offshore. Today, the computerization of work, widespread access to the Internet, and high-speed private data networks have allowed a wide range of knowledge-intensive jobs to become more footloose.[2]

Global outsourcing reveals many of the key features of contemporary globalization. It deals with international competitiveness in a way that underscores the growing interdependence of developed and developing countries; a huge part of the debate centres around jobs, wages and skills in different parts of the world; and there is a focus on how economic activities are organized

---

1     Much of the material discussed in these lectures reflects a close collaboration with John Humphrey (Institute of Development Studies, University of Sussex, UK) and Timothy Sturgeon (Industrial Performance Center, Massachusetts Institute of Technology, Cambridge, Mass., USA) as part of our joint work on the Global Value Chains Initiative funded by the Rockefeller Foundation in New York, NY. Information about this project can be found at http://www.globalvaluechains.org. However, the opinions or any errors contained in this publication are the sole responsibility of the author.

2     The extent of global outsourcing is impressive. In 2001, about 90 per cent of all consumer electronics sold in the United States were produced offshore, as were 80-85 per cent of footwear, toys, luggage and handbags, watches, clocks, games, and television sets, 70 per cent of bicycles, 60 per cent of computers, and 57 per cent of apparel (USITC, 2002).

across firms and country boundaries, and where in this production chain value and employment is created. There are enormous political as well as economic stakes in how global outsourcing plays itself out in the coming years, particularly as well-endowed and strategically positioned economies increase their participation in global value chains. Countries such as China, India, Mexico, the Philippines, Russia, and parts of Eastern and Central Europe are replete with college graduates who speak Western languages, have technical training in engineering and the sciences, and can handle outsourced information-technology work.

The rise of global outsourcing has triggered waves of consternation in advanced economies about job loss and the degradation of capabilities that could spell the disappearance of entire national industries. Many have dismissed these concerns, arguing instead that global outsourcing should be embraced as a mechanism for economies to shift out of low-value activities and old industries, freeing up capital and human resources for higher-value activities and the development of newer industries and cutting-edge products (*The Economist*, 2004a; 2004b). But clearly such assurances are of little comfort to those whose economic survival has been placed in jeopardy by direct competition with firms and workers with low wages and good skills.

Global outsourcing has also triggered a debate about the benefits and costs of globalization for developing countries. Some claim that it has been extremely beneficial, while others argue that global outsourcing has led only to "immiserizing" growth and a "race to the bottom," as developing countries compete with one another to offer transnational companies the lowest operating costs (Kaplinsky, 2000; 2005). The recent emergence of China and India as important nodes of activity – or hubs – in global value chains has expanded the global labour force so significantly that globalization may bid down the living standards not only for unskilled work and primary products, but increasingly for skilled work and industrial products as well.

Despite popular notions to the contrary, global outsourcing has not meant a wholesale transfer of economic activity out of developed economies and into developing ones. A large and important set of activities have remained rooted, at least so far, in advanced economies, even as they have become tightly linked to activities located elsewhere. The cumulative effect is that cross-border linkages between economies and firms have grown more elaborate. Firms are less likely to simply make products and export them; they increasingly participate in highly complex cross-border arrangements that involve a wide array of partners, customers, and suppliers. Global outsourcing has given rise to a new set of economic structures in the world economy that we refer to as "global value chains" (Gereffi and Kaplinsky, 2001; Gereffi et al., 2005).

In these lectures, the global value chains perspective is used to look at how offshore outsourcing has affected the quantity and quality of jobs in the

2

global economy. There are four main themes that run through the ILO Social Policy Lectures this year. First, an analysis of jobs in the contemporary global economy requires an integrated framework that looks at the industrial structures of both advanced industrial and developing economies, which are closely linked through the dynamics of global value chains. The strategies of new types of lead firms in these chains since the 1970s (global retailers, branded marketers, and brand-name manufacturers) have tied what is sometimes referred to as the deindustrialization or "hollowing out" of manufacturing sectors in developed countries to export-oriented industrialization in many parts of the developing world.

Second, jobs in the global economy are most usefully conceptualized not by their location in particular industries or countries, but rather by their role in global value chains. This paper discusses four types of jobs in the global economy: (1) assembly jobs, usually involving the processing of imported inputs for export of diverse manufactured products; (2) manufacturing jobs associated with the "full-package" production of finished consumer goods, typically led by US and European retailers and branded marketers in a process of buyer-oriented industrial upgrading; (3) jobs related to original design manufacturing (ODM) and own brand manufacturing (OBM), which often involve the supply of key components or subassemblies to large manufacturers in a process of supplier-oriented industrial upgrading; and (4) knowledge-intensive jobs linked to the offshore provision of research and development, information technology and business process services.

Third, while contemporary globalization has been associated with the geographical dispersion and fragmentation of production and trade networks, there has been a significant consolidation of global value chains in recent years. These consolidation trends will be illustrated with reference to China, India, and the apparel industry.

Fourth, and finally, we believe that these features of global value chains, industrial upgrading, and the global labour market highlight the need for a rethinking of the development agenda in both the developing and advanced industrial economies. This is driven not only by changes in the capabilities of countries and workers participating in the global economy, but also by pressures from transnational civil society actors to redefine and expand our contemporary notions of global corporate social responsibility and private as well as public governance.

## Offshore outsourcing and development: Old and new trends

Offshore outsourcing has been gathering pace since the 1970s. This process combines two quite distinct phenomena. "Outsourcing" is a standard aspect of all businesses, which frequently and continually need to make the decision to "make or buy" specific inputs and services. While companies regularly decide whether they wish to produce goods and services "in house" or buy them from outside vendors, the tendency in recent years has shifted in the direction of "buy." Major manufacturers, such as the automakers General Motors, Ford, and Toyota, have spun off their huge internal parts divisions as independent suppliers (Delphi, Visteon, and Denso, respectively), and many businesses have outsourced a wide range of services, such as accounts receivable, insurance, and logistics, to specialized firms. In industries like electronics, manufacturing itself has become a service.

"Offshoring" refers to the decision to move the supply of goods and services from domestic to overseas locations. These activities may be carried out in facilities owned in whole or in part by the parent firm, by transnational suppliers, or by local suppliers. The geographic shift of industries is certainly not a new phenomenon. In the early twentieth century in the United States, many industries that were established in New England, such as textiles, apparel, footwear and furniture, began to move to the US South in search of abundant natural resources and cheaper labour, frequently in "right to work" states that made it difficult to establish labour unions. The same forces behind the impetus to shift production to low-cost regions within the United States eventually led US manufacturers to cross national borders to places such as Japan, Mexico and Singapore, and eventually to most of East Asia. Another major driver of industry relocation have been trade rules, which either tilted the balance for market access in favour of local production or reduced tariffs in outward processing trade (or production sharing) to the point where manufacturing offshore for the home market became highly attractive.

The offshoring of jobs is not a new trend. It reflects the fragmentation and geographical expansion of international production and trade networks in the global economy, which has been going on for decades. The global value chains perspective highlights the various forms of explicit coordination or governance in global industries, and the existence of "new drivers" (most notably, retailers and branded marketers) in a wide range of agricultural, manufacturing, and service industries (see Gereffi et al., 2005; Gereffi, 2005).

From the point of view of global development, the offshoring of both manufacturing and service jobs is important because it has helped to spur the industrialization and upgrading processes that have occurred in developing countries. This has been one of the main positive aspects of globalization. But

4

a closer look at the kinds of jobs being created in global value chains reveals striking asymmetries and knowledge gaps.

## Jobs in the global economy: A global value chains perspective

From a global value chains perspective, the industrial structures of the advanced countries are intrinsically linked with networks of suppliers and workers across the world. A striking feature of contemporary globalization is that a very large and growing proportion of the workforce in many global value chains is now located in developing economies. In a phrase, the centre of gravity of much of the world's industrial production has shifted from the North to the South of the global economy. In the 1970s and 1980s, many of the newly industrializing economies were narrowing the industrialization gap with advanced economies, and by the end of the twentieth century, the proportion of gross domestic product (GDP) in manufacturing was actually higher in various parts of the developing world than in advanced industrial regions[3] (Arrighi et al., 2003).

These aggregate figures only tell part of the jobs and development story, however, and they hide deep and pervasive asymmetries in the global economy. First, the trend toward industrial convergence noted above was due primarily to First World de-industrialization, rather than to endogenously generated industrial development in the Third World. The shift of manufacturing jobs from developed economies to lower-cost production sites overseas entails what some see as a "hollowing out" of the industrialized world, including the growth of a vast service sector that accounts for two-thirds to three quarters of the jobs in high-wage economies, such as Canada, Germany, Japan, the United Kingdom and the United States (see figure 1.1). Thus, the offshoring of manufacturing jobs from industrialized nations is a key factor in explaining the impetus behind recent Third World industrialization.

Second, the gains from industrial growth are highly concentrated in both the developed and developing portions of the world. If we look at manufacturing value added (MVA) as an indicator of the amount of industrial activity actually carried out in different countries, the top three performers in

---

[3] The percentage of GDP in manufacturing in the Third World moved from 78.3 per cent of the First World average in 1970 to 99.4 per cent in 1980, 108.1 per cent in 1990 and 118 per cent in 1998. There was considerable unevenness at the regional level. Thus, in 1998, China was at 190 per cent of the First World average, Japan was at 119 per cent, East Asia (without China and Japan) at 130 per cent, and Latin America at 105 per cent. On the other extreme, West Africa and North Africa were just over 70 per cent of First World manufacturing levels, Sub-Saharan Africa stood at 78 per cent, and South Asia at 79 per cent (Arrighi et al., 2003, p. 12).

**Figure 1.1. Share of employment by economic sector in percentage, 2003**

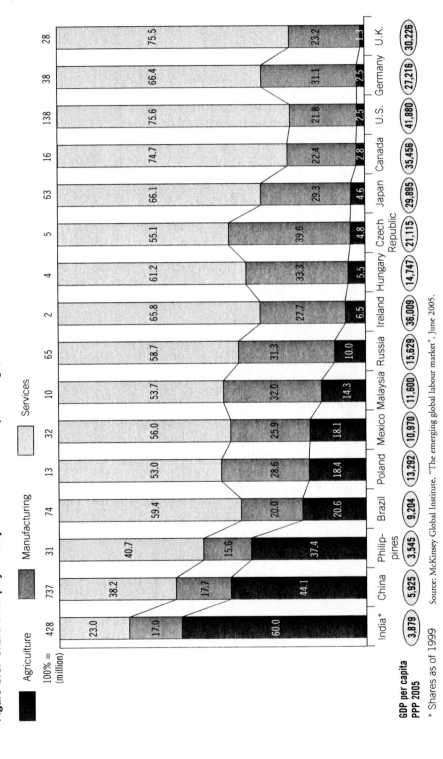

Source: McKinsey Global Institute, "The emerging global labour market", June 2005.

* Shares as of 1999

**Table 1.1. Shares of top ten economies, global manufacturing value added, 2003**

| Rank | All economies | Share in world (%) | Developing economies | Share in developing economies (%) |
|---|---|---|---|---|
| 1 | United States | 23.3 | China | 28.9 |
| 2 | Japan | 18.2 | Korea, Rep. of | 14.1 |
| 3 | Germany | 7.4 | Brazil | 8.8 |
| 4 | China | 6.9 | India | 5.1 |
| 5 | France | 4.5 | Mexico | 4.7 |
| Top 5 ranks | | 60.3 | Top 5 ranks | 61.6 |
| 6 | Italy | 3.4 | Thailand | 3.9 |
| 7 | Korea, Rep. of | 3.4 | Indonesia | 3.7 |
| 8 | United Kingdom | 3.2 | Argentina | 2.7 |
| 9 | Brazil | 2.1 | Turkey | 2.4 |
| 10 | Canada | 1.9 | Malaysia | 2.3 |
| Top 10 ranks | | 74.3 | Top 10 ranks | 76.6 |

Source: UNIDO, Online Country Database (http://www.unido.org/data/regions.cfm). Last accessed, 27 June 2006.

2003 in terms of their share of global MVA are the United States (23.3 per cent of the total), Japan (18.2 per cent), and Germany (7.4 per cent), followed by China (6.9 per cent). Within the developing world, just six economies account for nearly two-thirds of all MVA in 2003: China (28.9 per cent), Republic of Korea (14.1 per cent), Brazil (8.8 per cent), India (5.1 per cent), Mexico (4.7 per cent), and Thailand (3.9 per cent) (see table 1.1). Thus, most job creation and job shifts in manufacturing are occurring among a relative handful of dynamic developed and developing economies.

While the increase in the manufacturing GDP in developing economies is an aggregate indicator of development, it doesn't tell us anything about the types of jobs that exist in these industries. If we look at the leading exporters of high-technology products in 2003, we find six developing economies – China, Hong Kong (China), Singapore, Republic of Korea, Mexico, and Malaysia – among the top twelve countries worldwide, and China is number three worldwide with 8.8 per cent of global high technology exports (see table 1.2). What we do not know from these statistics, however, are the kinds of specific jobs within high-technology industries that are located in each country, as well as the kinds of companies that are providing these jobs. The same country could be exporting clothes, cars, and computers, but the trade

**Table 1.2. Top 15 exporters of high-technology products, 2003**

| Rank | Country | Exports (US $ billion) | World Total (%) |
|---|---|---|---|
| 1 | United States | 236.4 | 13.8 |
| 2 | Germany | 157.8 | 9.2 |
| 3 | China | 150.3 | 8.8 |
| 4 | Japan | 137.6 | 8.0 |
| 5 | Hong Kong (China) | 93.3 | 5.5 |
| 6 | France | 85.9 | 5.0 |
| 7 | Singapore | 81.1 | 4.7 |
| 8 | United Kingdom | 77.0 | 4.5 |
| 9 | Republic of Korea | 74.5 | 4.4 |
| 10 | Netherlands | 63.7 | 3.7 |
| 11 | Mexico | 57.5 | 3.4 |
| 12 | Malaysia | 54.7 | 3.2 |
| 13 | Belgium | 44.5 | 2.6 |
| 14 | Italy | 42.2 | 2.5 |
| 15 | Ireland | 39.7 | 2.3 |
| TOP 15 | | 1 396.2 | 81.7 |
| World | | 1 709.5 | 100.0 |

\* Definitions of "high-technology exports" are derived from the UNIDO Industrial Development Reports, on which this table is based. This includes SITC codes 524, 54, 712, 716, 718, 75, 761, 764, 771, 774, 776, 778, 792, 871, 874, 881 from SITC Revision 2. For more information, see UNIDO's 2005 Industrial Development Report (http://www.unido.org/file-storage/download/?file_id=44686).

Source: UN Comtrade Database (http://unstats.un.org/unsd/comtrade/). Last accessed 27 June, 2006.

data alone do not tell us whether the economy is carrying out labour-intensive assembly activities, advanced manufacturing of components and finished products, or product development, design, and engineering services. Nor do we know whether the main suppliers of these products are state companies, foreign-invested enterprises, or domestic firms. Yet it is precisely these details about types of jobs that are essential for us to evaluate development trajectories.

## The contemporary global labour market: A changing landscape

Usually when we think of jobs, we envision them as tied to particular individuals, places and industries. However, global value chains have created a new kind of global labour market that is tied to the demand for jobs in production, design, marketing, logistics and finance that cut *across* industries. Relatively unskilled farm and factory work has been moving offshore for decades. Recently, there have been unprecedented increases in the supply of offshore pools of low-wage, technically skilled workers in both manufacturing and services (Roach, 2003; Polaski, 2004).

Several factors underlie these shifts in the size and composition of the global labour market. First, following the break-up of the former Soviet Union in 1989 and the end of the Cold War, about 3 billion workers from China, India, Russia, and Eastern Europe – half of the world's labour force – joined the capitalist world economy, creating a labour supply shock on a scale unlike anything experienced before. Second, technological changes associated with the Internet allowed a dramatic expansion of outsourcing and offshoring options in services as well as manufacturing, and this real-time connectivity has converted what were once segmented national labour markets into an integrated, global production system. Third, transnational corporation business strategies have been unrelenting in their search for new efficiencies, especially on the labour side where substantial cost gains can be found.[4] As a result, offshore outsourcing is no longer considered merely an option, but "an increasingly urgent survival tactic for companies in the developed economies" (Roach, 2003, p. 6).

Global value chains encompass the full range of economic activities that are required to bring a good or service from conception through the different stages of production, delivery to final consumers, and final disposal after use (Kaplinsky, 2000; Gereffi and Kaplinsky, 2001). As such, they have given rise to different kinds of jobs in the global economy.[5] We distinguish four main types of jobs in this analysis: (1) assembly jobs in export-oriented industries, based on imported inputs; (2) basic manufacturing jobs associated with "full package" (or OEM) production[6] and buyer-oriented upgrading; (3) more advanced stages of manufacturing that require design (ODM) and brand (OBM) capabilities, which tend to be linked to supplier-oriented upgrading; and (4) the shift to offshoring of services, which include traditional white-

---

[4]   In the United States, worker compensation makes up nearly 80 per cent of total domestic corporate income, while wage rates in China and India are as low as 10 per cent of those for comparable quality workers in the United States and other developed countries (Roach, 2003, p. 5).

[5]   This classification scheme is not intended to refer to all jobs in the global economy; rather, it only applies to jobs linked to the offshore production of goods and services. Our main objective is to use the position of jobs in different types of global value chains to highlight features associated with trends in the creation, mobility and loss of these jobs.

[6]   While the precise definition of original equipment manufacturing (OEM) is subject to controversy (Sturgeon, 2001; Fuller, 2005, p. 290, fn. 9), the purpose of using the OEM, ODM, and OBM categories is to denote distinct production roles within global value chains – referring to manufacturing, design, and marketing competencies, respectively. For a fuller discussion of these roles in terms of upgrading dynamics, see Gereffi (1999; 2005), Sturgeon and Lester (2004), and Sturgeon and Lee (2005)

9

collar jobs and also more advanced activities associated with research and development and business process outsourcing.

## Assembly jobs in the global economy

The fragmentation of production that began in the 1960s and 1970s generated a search for labour-intensive assembly jobs in predominantly low-wage economies. Assembly jobs were usually the first stage of export-oriented industrialization in developing nations, and they tended to have a relatively large and positive impact on job creation, especially for female workers. Small, less-developed economies often specialize in particular export products, such as apparel, sporting goods, or electronics, while larger countries (such as China or Mexico) carry out assembly jobs in a more diversified range of industries. Sri Lanka, for example, generated 350,000 assembly jobs in the export-oriented apparel industry, which was the largest source of manufacturing employment in the country (ILO, 2003, p. 6).

Assembly jobs are often located in export-processing zones (EPZs). These sites have been established since the 1960s to attract foreign investment, boost employment, increase exports, and generate foreign exchange by providing factories, modern infrastructure, and streamlined administrative procedures ("one-stop shopping"). Table 1.3 shows several notable trends regarding the expansion of EPZs between 1975 and 2002. In 1975 there were close to 80 EPZs in 25 countries; by 1995 the number of countries with EPZs had nearly tripled to 73 and the number of EPZs grew more than sixfold to 500. In 2002, there were 3,000 EPZs in 116 countries. In terms of employment, the number of workers in EPZs roughly doubled from 22.5 million in 1997 to 43 million in 2002, with China alone accounting for 70-80 per cent of the global EPZ workforce – approximately 30-35 million workers (see table 1.3).

Why has the number of EPZs grown so rapidly?[7] Many early exporters such as the Republic of Korea, Mexico and Taiwan (China), dispensed with the EPZ model relatively quickly, and allowed generalized export incentives to all companies located in their economies. But table 1.3 indicates that EPZs have grown even more rapidly since 1995 than before that date. This suggests that assembly jobs continue to play a vital role in the global economy, and the large number of EPZs may actually be one of the best measures of the growth of global value chains. EPZs are useful in attracting investors, ramping up output, and meeting international standards for a variety of export products.

---

[7] There are different varieties of EPZs, such as Free Trade Zones (Dominican Republic), China's Special Economic Zones (SEZs), and Mexico's maquiladora sector.

**Table 1.3. The development of export processing zones**

|  | 1975 | 1986 | 1995 | 1997 | 2002 |
|---|---|---|---|---|---|
| No. of countries with EPZs | 25 | 47 | 73 | 93 | 116 |
| No. of EZPs | 79 | 176 | 500 | 845 | 3 000 |
| Employment (millions) | n.a. | n.a. | n.a. | 22.5 | 43 |
|   – of which China | n.a. | n.a. | n.a. | 18 | 30 |
|   – other countries<br>   for which figures available | 0.8 | 1.9 | n.a. | 4.5 | 13 |
| Total countries for which data<br>were available (108) |  |  |  |  |  |

Source: International Labour Office, "Employment and social policy in respect to export processing zones," GB.286/ESP/3, March 2003.

However, assembly jobs are also highly vulnerable to fluctuations in developed country demand, competition from other low-wage countries, and the purchasing preferences of lead firms in global value chains. Employment in Mexico's *maquiladora* industry, which assembles products for the US market based on imported inputs, rose from 446,000 in 1990 to 1,285,000 in 2000, but then fell to 1,086,000 workers in May 2002 due to a mild recession in the US economy, as well as intensified competition from China. Similarly, assembly jobs in the Dominican Republic fell from 200,000 in 2000 to 175,000 just one year later (ILO, 2003, p. 6). Thus, while the assembly role has created many jobs in the global economy, these tend to be low paying and footloose jobs, characterized by minimal local linkages to the host economy and poor working conditions. As a result, many developing economies are trying to move beyond assembly to more stable forms of integration with global value chains.

## Full-package production jobs and buyer-oriented upgrading

One of the most striking new features of the contemporary global economy has been the rise of "global buyers." These agents of globalization include giant discount chains, department stores, supermarkets, and brand marketers (so-called "manufacturers without factories"), who frequently drive the organization of global value chains (see Gereffi, 1994; 2005; Dolan and Humphrey, 2000). These retailers and marketers turned supply-side economics on its head, and played a direct role in shaping international production from the demand side, specifying which firms would make what products, how, where, when, and at what cost. Global buyers became gatekeepers to developed country markets, and they also shaped upgrading dynamics in developing economies.

The penchant of global buyers for the offshore production of consumer goods precipitated a dramatic flood of imports in developed countries, which were coupled with a steep decline in domestic employment in traditional manufacturing industries. East Asian manufacturers such as Hong Kong (China), Republic of Korea, Taiwan (China) and the Philippines focused on the OEM production of consumer goods, according to the designs and brand name specified by the buyer (Gereffi, 1999). Branded manufacturers also became "global buyers" to the extent that they outsourced production to low-cost offshore locations.

The key difference between assembly jobs and OEM jobs, the first two categories in our typology, is who supplies the inputs and coordinates the production process: in assembly production, developed country manufacturers control the inputs and the orders; in full-package or OEM production, global buyers in developed economies control the orders, but developing country suppliers coordinate the supply of inputs, make the final product, and send it to the buyers.[8]

A detailed study of the impact of offshore production shifts on the US economy by Bronfenbrenner and Luce (2004) illustrates in considerable detail the number and kinds of jobs involved, and who gains from these production shifts. Between 1992 and 2000, the authors estimate that each year between 70,000 and 100,000 production jobs moved from the United States to China and Mexico (Bronfenbrenner and Luce, 2004, p. 3, p. 17).

More detailed calculations for the first quarters of 2001 and 2004 indicate a significant increase in annual job losses from production shifts out of the United States during this three-year period. In 2001, the annual rate of job loss to both China and Mexico, extrapolated from first-quarter results, was 85,000 jobs going to each country, and 204,000 production jobs leaving the United States overall. By 2004, total US job losses due to offshore production shifts had doubled to 406,000, of which 140,000 went to Mexico, 99,000 to China, and 47,000 to India (Bronfenbrenner and Luce, 2004, p. 55).

Large diversified economies such as China, India and Mexico have been the main destinations for offshore production shifts from the United States. Each of these countries attracts a different mix of industries. China was the

---

[8] The performance standards for the goods and services that global buyers procure from their offshore suppliers in global value chains have tended to become more stringent and comprehensive over time. For instance, Wal-Mart requires all of its suppliers to hold their own inventory and to develop sophisticated electronic data interfaces with the giant retailer so that the regular replenishment of individual stores is guaranteed. Suppliers in Hong Kong (China) provide logistics, financial, and product development services that firms in other developing economies can't match. Thus, "full-package" production and buyer-oriented upgrading are often moving targets.

preferred location for the broadest range of industries: it captured all production shifts for sporting goods and toys; 40 per cent of production in electronics and electrical equipment, apparel and footwear; and one-third of US production shifts in aerospace, appliances, household goods, and wood and paper products. Mexico won out in a different set of industries: auto parts (68 per cent of US shifts), plastics, glass and rubber (58 per cent), appliances (56 per cent), industrial equipment and machinery (53 per cent), and wood and paper products (50 per cent). Meanwhile, India accounted for all US production shifts in finance, insurance, and real estate, and one-third of those in communications and information technology (Bronfenbrenner and Luce, 2004, p. 29).

## Advanced production jobs: Supplier-oriented upgrading and industry co-evolution

A different set of offshore activities emerged in the 1980s and 1990s as lead firms in capital- and technology-intensive value chains, such as automobiles and electronics, set up international production networks not only to assemble their finished goods, but also to develop a supply base for key intermediate products and sub-assemblies. At the uppermost tiers of these production networks, the suppliers tend to be very large and technologically sophisticated. Global contract manufacturers in electronics and mega-suppliers in the motor vehicles industry have established an international presence that has different implications for jobs and industrial upgrading than was characteristic of the labour-intensive, buyer-driven value chains.

The consolidation and geographic expansion of global suppliers have been dramatic. In electronics, the top five global contract manufacturers – Solectron, Flextronics, Sanmina/SCI, Celestica, and Jabil Circuit – increased their total revenues from $6.6 billion in 1994 to $56.4 billion in 2001 (Sturgeon and Lester, 2004, p. 47). This came about largely as a result of acquisitions of outsourced manufacturing plants from the large brand-name electronics companies like IBM, Hewlett-Packard, Lucent, Cisco Systems, Alcatel, and Ericsson. These US and European brand-name lead firms in electronics expect the global contract manufacturers not only to meet their full range of functional needs,[9] but also to provide these services all over the world. In motor vehicles, the process is similar. First-tier suppliers like Bosch, Johnson

---

[9]  In addition to excellent manufacturing performance, suppliers must be able to provide a wide range of value-enhancing services, such as product and component design, inventory management, product testing, packaging, and inbound and outbound logistics.

[10]  Consolidation has occurred largely through the acquisition of second-tier suppliers. It is estimated that 75 per cent of the value of a car can be accounted for by only 15 modules or sub-assemblies, such the suspension system, doors, dashboards, and drive trains (Sturgeon and Lester, 2004, p. 56).

Controls, Lear, Siemens Automotive, Magna, TRW, Denso, and others have attained both supply-chain consolidation[10] and a global footprint to meet the needs of the world's leading motor vehicle companies. In other words, these transnational manufacturers have created a new global supply base, which in turn creates both opportunities and challenges for local suppliers (Sturgeon and Lester, 2004).

The opportunities for local suppliers are related to the process of supplier-oriented upgrading and "industry co-evolution" described by Sturgeon and Lee (2005), which can improve technology learning and knowledge spillovers between developed and developing economies. A good example is the co-evolution of electronics contract manufacturing in Taiwan (China) and the United States. Lead firms in the global computer industry, such as Hewlett Packard/Compaq, Dell, Apple, and IBM, have relied heavily on Taiwanese contract manufacturers to supply their notebook and desktop personal computers, monitors, motherboards, optical disk drives, and servers. In the early 1990s, Taiwanese suppliers, known as "original design manufacturers" (ODMs), began to provide design services along with volume production, and some local companies, like Acer, created their own brand of personal computers as well. This form of supplier-oriented industrial upgrading created both jobs and enhanced technological capabilities for Taiwanese computer hardware suppliers.[11]

This model of supplier-oriented upgrading also has some negative implications for jobs in the developing world. First, industry co-evolution drives consolidation in the global supply base. Large and technologically sophisticated suppliers tend to concentrate "good" jobs in relatively few locations. The hard disk drive industry illustrates this pattern. Jobs in the US hard disk drive industry migrated to South-east Asia over a 20-year period beginning in the late 1970s. By the mid-1990s, 80 per cent of the jobs shifted to Singapore and other countries in South-east Asia, such as Malaysia. Nevertheless, hard disk drive design remained rooted in the United States, and since design jobs pay much more than production jobs, nearly 80 per cent of the wage bill was paid to workers in the United States, despite the fact that 80 per cent of the jobs were in South-east Asia (McKendrick et al., 2000).

Another problem is that supplier-oriented upgrading has a built-in contradiction. The automakers and electronics lead firms are reluctant to have

---

11    Another example of supplier-oriented upgrading and industry co-evolution involves the interplay between US brand name electronics firms, Taiwan's pure-play foundries (which do volume manufacturing of integrated circuits), and Taiwan's "fabless" semiconductor design industry, which is the second largest in the world after the United States (Fuller, 2005).

their suppliers learn too much, and thereby undercut the power of lead firms to set the knowledge parameters essential for product innovation. As a result, OEM and ODM suppliers are often limited by their customers to focus only on detailed design and production activities (Sturgeon and Lee, 2005, pp. 53-54). They are not encouraged to develop more profitable production of own brands or engage in breakthrough research and development activities.

## Knowledge-intensive jobs in offshore services

The outsourcing debate in the United States ratcheted up its intensity level in 2003 when the spectre of "white-collar outsourcing" was unveiled in a *Business Week* cover story, "Is your job next?" (Engardio et al., 2003). While low-cost offshore production had been displacing US factory and farm jobs for decades, the idea that middle-class office work and many high-paying professions were now subject to international competition came as something of a shock. The news got even worse when outsourcing was reputed to endanger the two strongholds of developed country value chain supremacy: design (Rocks and Moon, 2004) and innovation (Engardio and Einhorn, 2005). In his bestseller, *The world is flat*, Thomas Friedman (2005) lauded the rapid progress of India and China in upgrading to relatively high value activities in service and manufacturing global value chains, and he challenged the advanced industrial economies to sustain their competitive edge through innovation and the creation of new waves of knowledge-intensive jobs.

Facts regarding the current extent of the offshoring of services don't come easily. The best known study of service sector outsourcing to date is by a business consulting firm, the McKinsey Global Institute (2005). It argues that outsourcing in the service sector is generally beneficial to the US economy, and far less detrimental to jobs than outsourcing in the manufacturing sector has been. According to the report, only 11 per cent, or 160 million, of the 1.46 billion service jobs around the world could be performed remotely, and just a small fraction of those jobs will actually go offshore. [12] The jobs most amenable to remote employment are engineering (a 52 per cent likelihood) and finance and accounting (31 per cent).

McKinsey's study identified a series of supply-side constraints that indicate that, on average, just 13 per cent of the 33 million university graduates in the 28 low-wage nations included in the study are suitable for jobs in multinational corporations from developed countries (Farrell et al., 2005). The 83 human-resource managers for multinationals in low-wage countries who were

---

[12]  McKinsey estimated that in 2003, only 1.5 million service jobs were done in low-wage countries for clients in higher-wage countries, and by 2008, this number is expected to reach 4.1 million - just 1.2 per cent of the total number of service jobs in developed countries.

interviewed for the study cited a variety of reasons for this shortfall, including: a lack of language skills (especially English); an emphasis in their training on theory over practical knowledge; an inadequate appreciation of the importance of teamwork and flexible work; and locational disadvantages (many university graduates live far from major cities with international airline connections). Despite the relatively small number of people presently involved in the off-shoring of services, the McKinsey study argues that this trend is permanent and it can be expected to grow significantly, especially in key locations like China, India and the Philippines.

The International Monetary Fund (IMF) also takes a sanguine view of this phenomenon, claiming that "the risk of service outsourcing dramatically reducing job growth in the advanced economies has been greatly exaggerated" (Amiti and Wei, 2004, p. 20). Using data for 2002, the study finds that the top outsourcers of business services are the United States (US$41 billion) and Germany (US$39 billion), followed by Japan (US$25 billion), the Netherlands ($21 billion), Italy ($20 billion), France ($19 billion), and the United Kingdom ($16 billion). However, many of these same countries were also the biggest recipients of business services from abroad in 2002: the United States ($59 billion), the United Kingdom ($37 billion), Germany ($28 billion), France ($21 billion), and the Netherlands ($20 billion) (Amiti and Wei, 2004, pp. 13-15). Therefore, the IMF study claims that the anxiety concerning serv-ice sector outsourcing is misplaced because many developed countries, such as the United States and the United Kingdom, run sizable surpluses in business services with the rest of the world.

Neither the McKinsey Global Institute report nor the IMF study are likely to assuage the major concerns of service sector workers in developed countries. From the perspective of multinational companies, the offshoring of business services is efficiency-enhancing and profitable. It continues the trend toward fragmentation and specialization in global value chains, and offshore suppliers can be added to the set of winners that benefit from globalization. However, the tendency toward global consolidation applies to knowledge-intensive jobs as well as those in manufacturing. Thus, the real concern is whether there are forces in the global economy that can effectively disseminate the employment gains from globalization to a broader set of countries, or whether global consolidation among a handful of countries and suppliers will be exacerbated.

# Lecture 2. Global consolidation and industrial upgrading: The promise and perils of development

## Introduction

There are fundamental changes afoot in the global economy, and no simple answers for countries that want to improve or even maintain their levels of development. In recent decades, both inward-oriented and outward-oriented development models have come under increasing scrutiny, and countries are trying to determine what kinds of policies and institutions provide the best opportunities for long-term growth and prosperity.

Since the mid-1980s, globalization has been associated with a neoliberal model of development that has produced rapid economic growth and improving standards of living in some parts of the world, most notably East Asia. In other regions, like Latin America, neoliberalism has been marked by slow economic growth, large-scale unemployment, social deterioration, and political protest (Dussel Peters, 2000; Lora et al., 2004). Development models in both Latin America and East Asia, however, have evolved considerably during this period.

Within the global economy, China, India and Mexico present particularly interesting cases because of their highly successful but divergent development models. Mexico is the most diversified and export-oriented economy in Latin America, with a heavy reliance on manufactured exports to the United States. China currently is one of the world's fastest growing economies, characterized by extensive economic diversification and booming exports to all parts of the world. Both Mexico and China rely heavily on foreign direct investment to fuel their export growth. India, by contrast, was until the early 1990s an inward-oriented economy, but it has now become a major player on the global economic stage, sparked to a large degree by the stellar performance of its information technology sector. However, unlike Mexico and China, India relies more extensively on home-grown entrepreneurs than foreign capital to spur development (see Huang and Khanna, 2003).

This lecture will provide an overview of two different trends in the global economy: consolidation and industrial upgrading. China and India have prompted a great deal of attention to the potential for global consolidation. This is a particular concern in the apparel industry, where the elimination of quotas at the end of 2004 threatens to terminate the guaranteed access that many small garment exporting nations had to developed country markets. At the same time, countries are preoccupied with industrial upgrading, or "moving up" in the global economy. We will examine this process in detail for Mexico and China, which have used international trade as a mechanism to try to promote their economic growth. Exports are key to the development strategies and employment dynamics of many smaller economies as well, so we will examine the potential and limits of certain kinds of upgrading within global value chains.

## Global consolidation: China, India and the apparel industry

To examine the employment implications of the trends toward consolidation in the global economy, we will examine the cases of China and India, as well as the shift from dispersion to growing concentration in the global apparel industry.

### China: The "Workshop of the world"

China stands at the centre of the story of offshore production because it has advanced so rapidly as the supplier of choice in virtually all labour-intensive global value chains. Whereas China had concentrated on a limited number of industries in the 1990s, "by 2001 an increasing percentage of the jobs shifting to China were in higher-end manufacturing of goods such as bicycles, furniture, motors, compressors, generators, fibre optics, injection molding, and computer components" (Bronfenbrenner and Luce, 2004, p. 4). Furthermore, China had attained a virtually insurmountable cost advantage in most consumer goods industries.[13] China's appeal is not merely to low-cost producers; it supplies all of the leading brand manufacturers that target the United States as well as global markets – Mattel Barbie Dolls, Levi jeans, Samsonite luggage, Rubbermaid kitchenware, Remington electric shavers, Carrier air conditions, and so on.

China's rise to global prominence marks a new phase of global consolidation. However, a global value chain perspective adds several important dimensions to the China story. First, China's emergence, like that of the other East Asian "miracle economies," is inextricably intertwined with the role of global buyers; it is demand-pull more than supply-push. A telling example is China's relationship with Wal-Mart, the world's largest retailer with sales of more than $245 billion in 2003. More than 80 per cent of the 6,000 factories in Wal-Mart's worldwide network of suppliers are in China. In 2003, Wal-Mart spent $15 billion on Chinese-made products; this total accounted for nearly one-eighth of all Chinese exports to the United States. If Wal-Mart were a separate nation, it would have ranked as China's fifth-largest export market, ahead of Germany and Britain (Goodman and Pan, 2004).

A second feature of the China story is the role of global intermediaries. About two-thirds of China's exports are shipped from factories wholly or jointly owned by foreign investors, mainly from Hong Kong, Taiwan (China), and Japan. It is reported, for example, that foreign-invested enterprises account for more than 85 per cent of China's high-technology exports, and for three-quarters of its sales of technology-related products abroad (Shenkar, 2005, p. 68). This is in striking contrast to India, where domestically owned firms are key to exports and offshore outsourcing in the information technology (IT) sector (Huang and Khanna, 2003).[14]

Third, China's reliance on global buyers and its "survival of the cheapest" approach has created a production glut that places enormous pressures on wages, working conditions, and profit margins at the factory level. A typical export factory in southern China pays a salary of $40 per month, which is 40 per cent less than the local minimum wage. Workers put in 18-hour days with poor workplace conditions, minimal training, and continual pressure to boost output (Wonacott, 2003).

Finally, China confronts a structural employment problem in consolidating its position atop the global manufacturing pyramid. In 2002, China's

---

[13] In furniture, for example, the vice president of marketing for a leading US manufacturer headquartered in North Carolina testified before the US Congress that a Chinese bedroom set comparable to his company's $22,750 offering was priced at $7,070, a saving of 69 per cent to the consumer (Shenkar, 2005, p. 106).

[14] The influence of global intermediaries extends well beyond China, however. In athletic footwear, for example, manufacturers based in the Republic of Korea and Taiwan (China) typically run the factories in Vietnam, Indonesia, Thailand, and China that supply shoes to Nike, Reebok, Adidas and all the other major brands. East Asian intermediaries play a similar role for export-oriented apparel suppliers in sub-Saharan Africa and the Caribbean Basin.

**Table 2.1. Number and share of workers in China's manufacturing industries, 1994-2000***

| Category | 1994 No. of workers (1,000) | Share (%) | 1996 No. of workers (1,000) | Share (%) | 1998 No. of workers (1,000) | Share (%) | 2000 No. of workers (1,000) | Share (%) |
|---|---|---|---|---|---|---|---|---|
| Manufacturing industry | 54 320 | 100.0 | 52 930 | 100.0 | 37 690 | 100.0 | 32 400 | 100.0 |
| Light industry | 18 060 | 33.3 | 17 280 | 32.7 | 11 650 | 30.9 | 9 950 | 30.7 |
| Chemical products | 7 960 | 14.7 | 8 140 | 15.4 | 6 220 | 16.5 | 5 350 | 16.5 |
| Metal products | 10 440 | 19.2 | 10 260 | 19.4 | 7 430 | 19.7 | 6 380 | 19.7 |
| Machinery | 10 810 | 19.9 | 10 560 | 20.0 | 7 510 | 19.9 | 6 290 | 19.4 |
| Electronics and telecommunications | 3 960 | 7.3 | 3 990 | 7.5 | 3 040 | 8.1 | 2 830 | 8.7 |
| Miscellaneous | 3 610 | 6.7 | 2 110 | 4.0 | 1 390 | 3.7 | 1 220 | 3.8 |

*Includes only state-owned industrial enterprises and non-state enterprises with annual sales greater than 5 million yuan.
Source: National Bureau of Statistics: *China Statistical Yearbook 2002*. Cited in Douglas Zhihua Zeng, "*China's employment, challenges and strategies after the WTO accession,*" World Bank Policy Research Working Paper No. 3522, Feb. 2005, p. 6.

labour force of nearly 750 million people accounted for over one-quarter of the world's total. It is estimated that China will have to create around 10 to 30 million jobs per year during the coming decade to absorb a multitude of laid off workers and rural emigrants as it shifts from an agricultural to an industrial economy, and soon to a knowledge- and service-based economy (Zeng, 2005). Despite an effective unemployment rate estimated to be at least 10 per cent, which has been a major cause of urban poverty and worsening inequality, China is facing significant labour shortages, especially in the light manufacturing industries that have accounted for much of the country's export growth.

Table 2.1 shows that between 1994 and 2000, the number of manufacturing workers in China declined from 54.3 million to 32.4 million, in large part as a result of the state sector shedding jobs in large numbers. The workforce in light, labour-intensive industries was nearly halved from 18 million workers to just under 10 million workers (30.7 per cent of manufacturing workers in 2000), while the much touted knowledge-intensive industries (electronics and telecommunications) do not generate many new jobs (just 8.7 per cent of the manufacturing labour force in 2000). In response to this situation, China is adopting a range of policies, including encouraging private sector growth, expanding the service sector, reforming state-owned enterprises, and establishing mass retraining programmes.

# India: The offshoring of information technology services

Offshore outsourcing in India's IT sector is considered by many as a globalization success story. In 2002 India's IT service providers were the dominant offshore vendors, delivering an estimated $10 billion in IT services (Karamouzis, 2003). India employs about 650,000 professionals in IT services, and this figure is expected to more than triple in the next five years [15] (Roach, 2003, p. 6). The significance of India as an offshore site for IT services is perhaps best represented by General Electric's "70-70-70" outsourcing rule of thumb: General Electric has publicly stated its goals of outsourcing 70 per cent of its work, moving 70 per cent of this outsourcing offshore, and locating 70 per cent of these IT jobs in India. Thus, about one-third of GE's IT work will be done in India.

While General Electric is a global pacesetter in India, lots of other big companies are moving in the same direction. The top five US employers in India are: General Electric with 17,800 workers, which is about 5.6 per cent of its global workforce of 315,000 people; Hewlett-Packard, 11,000 employees in India; IBM, 6,000 employees; American Express, 4,000 employees; and Dell, 3,800 employees (Pink, 2004, p. 13). While US firms have created as many as 100,000 IT jobs in India, a strong nucleus of domestic IT service providers there has emerged to handle this demand, including: Tata Consultancy Services – 23,400 employees and over $1 billion in revenues (as of March 2003); Wipro Technologies (19,800 employees and $690 million in revenues); Infosys Technologies (15,500 workers, over $750 million in revenues); and companies like Satyam Computer Services and HCL Technologies, with close to 10,000 employees each and $460 million and over $330 million in revenues, respectively (Karamouzis, 2003). [16]

From a global value chain perspective, many of the software and other IT jobs in India involve routine work on mainframe computers using relatively standardized or outmoded technology. However, the lure of the Indian subcontinent makes eminent sense for US companies, who see this as a win-win situation in economic terms. In the United States, gross domestic product per capita in 2003 was just over $35,000 and the typical salary for a programmer was $70,000; in India, GDP per capita was $480, and a typical programmer earned $8,000 per year (Pink, 2004, p. 13). Thus, Indian programmers make only one-ninth of their US counterparts, but in the domestic setting the Indian programmers are earning more than 16 times the minimum wage, while the

---

[15]  Of course, one or two million jobs, even if highly skilled and well paid, could appear insignificant in terms of India's total population of 1.2 billion people.

[16]  By March 2004, Infosys Technologies and Wipro reportedly both topped $1 billion in revenues for the first time (Rai, 2004).

average US programmer earns only twice the minimum wage. Furthermore, India is already beginning to offer higher-level services, such as systems architecture, design, and technology strategy services (Chadwick, 2003).

While IT outsourcing is viewed in a positive light by many in India, it has become a highly politicized and emotional issue in the United States. According to Vivek Paul, vice-chairman of Wipro Technologies, "If three million jobs have been lost in the United States, and 100,000 created in India, every one of those three million thinks, 'That's my job' " (Waldman, 2004). Unemployment in India is at its highest level in decades: officially pegged at 7 per cent, many economists believe the actual level is over 20 per cent. According to commentators in both the United States and India, IT outsourcing reveals not only the asymmetries of globalization, but the incredibly high stakes for developing as well as developed countries.

## Trade rules and global consolidation in apparel

International trade rules have an enormous influence on the creation and distribution of jobs in the global economy. One of the best examples is the Multifiber Arrangement (MFA) in the apparel value chain, which from the early 1970s until 1995 opened up the markets of the United States, Canada, and Western Europe to exports from a wide range of developing economies by placing quantitative limits (or quotas) on imports for a variety of textile and apparel products. As a result of these quotas, the North American and European textile and apparel markets received imports from 50 to 60 different developing economies (Gereffi and Memodovic, 2003).

The international spread of the apparel value chain has been well documented in various sources (Gereffi, 1999; UNCTAD, 2005). As seen in table 2.2, the leading apparel exporters in 1990 were concentrated in East Asia: China, Hong Kong (China), Republic of Korea and Taiwan (China). During the early 1990s, Thailand, Indonesia, Turkey, and India grew rapidly as apparel exporters, and after the passage of the North American Free Trade Agreement in 1994, Mexico became a star performer because of the rapid expansion of its exports to the US market. The biggest exporters of apparel tend to be relatively diversified economies, where apparel as a share of total national exports ranges from around 12 per cent to 16 per cent (China, India) to less than 5 per cent (Mexico, Republic of Korea, Thailand). However, the reliance on apparel exports is very high in some of the least developed economies, such as Bangladesh (77 per cent), Sri Lanka (51 per cent), and Tunisia and Morocco (about one-third of total exports). [17]

---

[17] There is a strong, but far from perfect, correlation between high levels of apparel exports and low wages. The reason for the disparity is that some countries with relatively high wages - Hong Kong (China), Republic of Korea and Taiwan (China) - play a major role because they still have access to large apparel quotas primarily issued by the United States and Western Europe.

## Table 2.2. World's top non-EU apparel exporters, 1990-2005

| Region/Country | Apparel exports to the world market (US$ billions) | | | | Apparel as per cent of total national exports | |
|---|---|---|---|---|---|---|
| | 1990 | 1995 | 2000 | 2005 | 1995 (%) | 2005 (%) |
| **North-east Asia** | | | | | | |
| China | 10.2* | 24.0 | 36.1 | 74.2 | 16.2 | 9.7 |
| Hong Kong (China) | 15.7* | 21.3 | 24.6 | 27.3 | 12.2 | 9.3 |
| Korea, Rep. of | 7.9 | 5.0 | 5.0 | 2.6 | 4.0 | 0.9 |
| Taiwan (China)* | 4.2* | 3.5* | 3.5* | n.a. | 2.8 | n.a. |
| **South-east Asia** | | | | | | |
| Indonesia | 1.6 | 3.4 | 4.7 | 5.1 | 7.4 | 6.0 |
| Thailand | 2.8 | 5.0 | 3.8 | 4.1 | 8.9 | 3.7 |
| Vietnam | 0.1* | 0.9* | 1.8 | 3.5[b] | 14.9 | 17.2[b] |
| Philippines | 0.7* | 1.1 | 2.5 | 2.3 | 6.1 | 5.5 |
| Malaysia | 1.3 | 2.3 | 2.3 | 2.3a | 3.1 | 1.8 |
| Cambodia | 0.0* | 0.1* | 1.0 | 2.0a | 16.3 | 70.8 |
| Singapore | 1.6 | 1.5 | 1.8 | 1.7 | 1.2 | 0.7 |
| **South Asia** | | | | | | |
| India | 2.5 | 4.1 | 6.2 | 6.6[a] | 13.0 | 8.3 |
| Bangladesh | 0.6 | 2.0 | 3.9 | 4.4[a] | 57.8 | 76.6 |
| Pakistan | 1.0 | 1.6 | 2.1 | 3.0[a] | 19.8 | 22.6 |
| Sri Lanka | 0.6 | 1.1* | 2.6* | 2.8[a] | 47.8 | 50.6 |
| **Central and Eastern Europe** | | | | | | |
| Turkey | 3.3 | 6.1 | 6.5 | 11.2a | 28.3 | 17.7 |
| Romania | 0.4 | 1.4 | 2.3 | 4.6 | 17.2 | 16.7 |
| Poland | 0.4* | 2.3 | 1.9 | 2.2[a] | 10.1 | 3.0 |
| Bulgaria | 0.1* | 0.4* | 0.7 | 1.8[a] | 7.9 | 17.7 |
| **Africa and the Middle East** | | | | | | |
| Tunisia | 1.1 | 2.3 | 2.2 | 3.3[a] | 42.4 | 34.0 |
| Morocco | 0.7* | 0.8 | 2.4 | 3.0[a] | 16.9 | 30.5 |
| Jordan | 0.01 | 0.03 | 0.1 | 1.1 | 1.6 | 24.8 |
| Mauritius | 0.6 | 0.8 | 0.9 | 0.9[a] | 52.5 | 48.8 |
| **North America** | | | | | | |
| Mexico | 0.0 | 2.7 | 8.6 | 7.3 | 3.4 | 3.4 |
| **World totals*** | **110.6*** | **168.7*** | **215.3*** | **n.a.** | **3.2** | **n.a.** |

* World Trade Analyzer (WTA), based on United Nations trade data. Apparel is defined as SITC 84.

[a] = 2004 UN Comtrade data; [b] = 2003 UN Comtrade data; n.a. = Not available.

Source: UN Comtrade. Apparel is defined as SITC 84.

However, in 1995 the World Trade Organization (WTO) issued an Agreement on Textiles and Clothing that mandated a 10-year phase out period for all MFA quotas.[18] There is great consternation among developing economies that the deregulation of apparel will contribute mightily to global consolidation in one of the world's most diversified export industries by allowing China in particular, along with other major suppliers like India, Indonesia, Pakistan, and Vietnam, to dominate US and European apparel markets. In the words of a definitive study by the US International Trade Commission on the impact of quota elimination in 2005: "China is expected to become the 'supplier of choice' for most US importers (the large apparel companies and retailers) because of its ability to make almost any type of textile and apparel product at any quality level at a competitive price" (USITC, 2004, p. xi).

The removal of apparel quotas is of grave concern to apparel and textile manufacturers in advanced industrial and developing countries alike. The main reason for concern in both cases is China. Estimates have been made of the impact of MFA quota elimination on the main sources of US apparel imports. Before quota elimination (in 2003), China had a 16 per cent share of the US apparel market, Mexico 10 per cent, the rest of the Americas 16 per cent, Hong Kong (China) 9 per cent, and India 4 per cent. After quota removal (2008), China's US apparel market share is expected to jump to 50 per cent, India to 15 per cent, Mexico to 3 per cent, and the rest of the Americas to 5 per cent (Nordås, 2004, p. 30).

Current US trade data from 2000 through 2005 show that these projections are not far off the mark. China increased its share of US apparel imports from 18.8 per cent in 2004 to 26.1 per cent in 2005, while Mexico's market share slipped from its top spot with 13.6 per cent of the total in 2000, down to 6.3 per cent in 2005 (see table 2.3).

In its report on the impact of quota elimination on developing countries, the USITC (2004) identified those countries whose apparel exports to the United States are highly concentrated in products most vulnerable to tight quota categories (i.e., knit shirts, pants, underwear, and pyjamas). These "highly concentrated producers" include: Lesotho (95 per cent), Jamaica (90 per cent), Honduras (86 per cent), Haiti (80 per cent), El Salvador (80 per cent), Kenya (77 per cent), and Nicaragua (76 per cent), with the percentages referring to the share of their total US apparel exports concentrated in the product categories most affected by quotas. Now that quotas have been removed in

---

[18]    Under specified cases of market disruption, the US market access agreement with China regarding its entry into the World Trade Organization allows the United States to apply selective safeguards (or quotas) on imports of Chinese textiles and apparel for four additional years beyond the termination of textile and apparel quotas for WTO members - that is, from 1 January 2005 to 31 December 2008. However, the agreement also states that no safeguards established during this four-year period will remain in effect beyond one year, without reapplication, unless both countries agree.

**Table 2.3. Top 7 apparel exporters to the United States, 2000-05**

| | 2000 | | 2001 | | 2002 | | 2003 | | 2004 | | 2005 | |
|---|---|---|---|---|---|---|---|---|---|---|---|---|
| | Export value (US$ bill) | % of total | Export value (US$ bill) | % of total | Export value (US$ bill) | % of total | Export value (US$ bill) | % of total | Export value (US$ bill) | % of total | Export value (US$ bill) | % of total |
| China | 8.5 | 13.2 | 8.9 | 13.9 | 9.6 | 15.0 | 11.4 | 16.7 | 13.6 | 18.8 | 19.9 | 26.1 |
| Mexico | 8.7 | 13.6 | 8.1 | 12.7 | 7.7 | 12.1 | 7.2 | 10.6 | 6.9 | 9.6 | 6.3 | 8.3 |
| Hong Kong | 4.6 | 7.1 | 4.3 | 6.7 | 4.0 | 6.2 | 3.8 | 5.6 | 3.9 | 5.4 | 3.6 | 4.7 |
| India | 2.0 | 3.1 | 1.9 | 3.0 | 2.1 | 3.2 | 2.2 | 3.2 | 2.4 | 3.3 | 3.1 | 4.1 |
| Indonesia | 2.2 | 3.4 | 2.4 | 3.7 | 2.2 | 3.4 | 2.2 | 3.3 | 2.5 | 3.4 | 3.0 | 3.9 |
| Vietnam | 0.05 | 0.1 | 0.05 | 0.1 | 0.9 | 1.4 | 2.4 | 3.5 | 2.6 | 3.6 | 2.7 | 3.6 |
| Honduras | 2.4 | 3.8 | 2.4 | 3.8 | 2.5 | 3.9 | 2.6 | 3.8 | 2.7 | 3.8 | 2.7 | 3.5 |
| **Total** | **64.3** | | **63.9** | | **63.8** | | **68.2** | | **72.3** | | **76.4** | |

Source: http://dataweb.usitc.gov, US Department of Commerce, US general imports, customs value. Accessed 3 March, 2006.

2005, these countries – among the poorest in the world – are the most vulnerable to precipitous job declines.

The apparel case shows another side of the competition for jobs in global value chains. Previously we have emphasized how offshore production shifts to large developing countries, like China and India, affect labour markets in the developed economies. In the apparel value chain, however, the most serious impact of China's and India's gains won't be felt in the United States or Europe, but in the developing economies that have relied on low wages and special access to developed country markets to sustain jobs and foreign exchange in what is for many their main export industry. Between 70 per cent and 80 per cent of workers in the apparel sector today are women in the poorest of countries (Nordås, 2004, p. 30). Without their jobs in the apparel industry, they are unlikely to find work in the formal sector of their economies. However, a return to protection is not likely to be the best option for improving the role of developing economies in global value chains.

## Industrial upgrading in Mexico and China – An international trade perspective

Industrial upgrading is defined as "the process by which economic actors – nations, firms, and workers – move from low-value to relatively high-value activities in global production networks" (Gereffi, 2005, p. 171). One of the ways that we can assess industrial upgrading for export-oriented economies such as China and Mexico is to look at shifts in the technology content of their exports over time. We divide each country's exports into five product groupings, which are listed in ascending levels of technological content: primary products, resource-based manufactures, and low- medium-, and high-technology manufactures.[19]

In figure 2.1, we see that in 1985, nearly 60 per cent of Mexico's total exports to the US market were primary products, the most important of which was oil. In 1993, one year prior to the establishment of NAFTA, medium-technology manufactures (mainly automotive products) and high-tech manufactures (largely electronics items) moved ahead of primary products in Mexico's export mix. By 2003, about two-thirds of Mexico's exports of $150 billion to the US market were in the medium- and high-technology product categories, followed by low-technology manufactures (such as textiles, apparel, and footwear). Thus, in less than 20 years, Mexico's export structure was transformed from one based on primary products to one dominated by medium- and high-technology manufactured items.

---

[19]  Sanjaya Lall (2000) developed this technological classification of exports based on 3-digit Standard International Trade Classification (SITC) categories. His article provides a detailed list of products under each category.

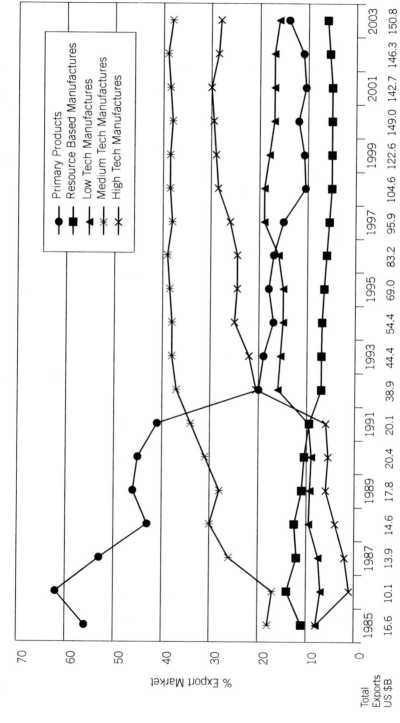

**Figure 2.1. Composition of Mexico's exports to the US market, 1985-2003**

Legend:
- Primary Products
- Resource Based Manufactures
- Low Tech Manufactures
- Medium Tech Manufactures
- High Tech Manufactures

% Export Market

| | 1985 | 1987 | 1989 | 1991 | 1993 | 1995 | 1997 | 1999 | 2001 | 2003 |
|---|---|---|---|---|---|---|---|---|---|---|
| Total Exports US $B | 16.6 10.1 | 13.9 14.6 | 17.8 20.4 | 20.1 38.9 | 44.4 54.4 | 69.0 83.2 | 95.9 104.6 | 122.6 149.0 | 142.7 146.3 | 150.8 |

Source: World Trade Analyzer, Statistics Canada.

27

In figure 2.2, we see the composition of China's exports to the US market during the same 1985-2003 period. Unlike Mexico, the leading product category in China's exports to the US market has consistently been low-technology manufactured goods. These were primarily made up of a wide variety of light consumer goods – apparel, footwear, toys, sporting goods, house wares, and so on. These products accounted for about two-thirds of China's overall exports to the United States in the mid-1990s. By 2003, however, high-technology exports from China had increased their share to nearly 40 per cent of China's overall exports to the US market, and, by the mid-2000s, were poised to pass low-technology exports for the top spot in China's export mix.

Mexico and China have a number of commonalities in their export trajectories to the US market since 1985. Both are diversified economies, with a range of different types of export products. In both cases, manufactured exports are more important than primary product or resource-based exports; within manufacturing, high- and medium-technology exports are displacing low-technology goods. While these export data have limitations as indicators of industrial upgrading,[20] both economies appear to be increasing the sophistication of their export structures.

A more detailed look at the international trade data, however, shows that since 2000, China has bested Mexico in head-to-head competition in the US market. Table 2.4 identifies six of the leading manufactured products in which China and Mexico are significant US suppliers. In five of these products, Mexico's share of the US market was greater than China's in 2000; by 2005, China had wrested the lead from Mexico in all but one of these items. In automatic data processing machines (SITC 752), for example, China's share of US imports quadrupled from 11.3 per cent in 2000 to 47.1 per cent in 2005. In telecommunications equipment (SITC 764), China's market share nearly tripled from 10.3 per cent to 28.9 per cent; and in electrical machinery (SITC 778), it doubled from 11.9 per cent to 22.1 per cent. Only in auto parts and accessories (SITC 784) did Mexico expand its lead in the US market over China.

Table 2.5 shows the top US imports in which either Mexico or China accounted for 20 per cent or more of the US market in 2005. Mexico had 10 products that met this criterion in 2005, whereas China had 24 such items.

---

[20]  The main problem with these export data is that they are not sufficiently detailed to tell us about the processes by which these products are elaborated. Auto parts or electronic components, for example, can be made in labour-intensive ways by relatively unskilled workers or they can be highly automated using capital-intensive technology. Thus, industrial upgrading cannot be assured just by moving in the direction of medium- or high-technology finished products. However, it is quite likely that the relative proportion of high-value activities and the skill level of jobs will increase as we move from low-technology to medium- and high-technology export categories. More precise cross-national and longitudinal occupational data are needed to explore this key research topic.

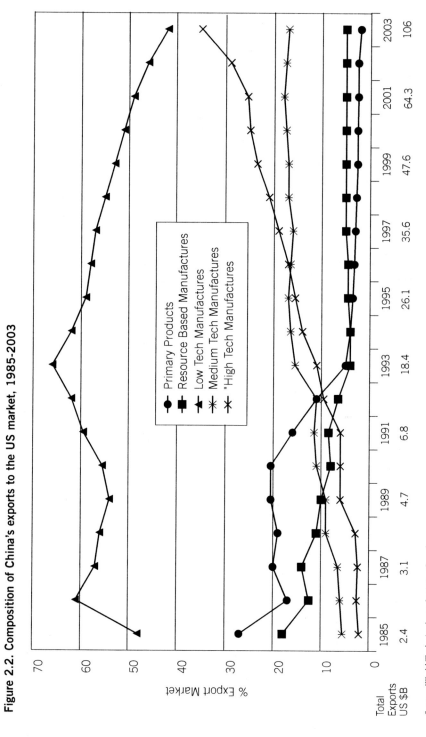

**Figure 2.2. Composition of China's exports to the US market, 1985-2003**

Source: World Trade Analyzer, Statistics Canada.

**Table 2.4. Competing exports by Mexico and China to the United States, 2000-05**

| SITC category | Product | | 2000 Value (US$ millions) | Share of US market | 2005 Value (US$ millions) | Share of US market | Change in US markets share 2000-05 |
|---|---|---|---|---|---|---|---|
| 752 | Automatic data processing machines and units | Mexico | 6 413 | 11.5 | 5 653 | 8.9 | –2.6 |
| | | China | 6 310 | 11.3 | 29 883 | 47.1 | +35.8 |
| | | **US Total** | **55 909** | | **63 465** | | |
| 764 | Telecommunications, equipments and parts | Mexico | 9 128 | 20.6 | 7 670 | 12.7 | –7.9 |
| | | China | 4 579 | 10.3 | 17 543 | 28.9 | +18.6 |
| | | **US Total** | **44 349** | | **60 625** | | |
| 778 | Electrical machinery and apparatus | Mexico | 3 144 | 18.3 | 4 363 | 21.8 | +3.5 |
| | | China | 2 040 | 11.9 | 4 414 | 22.1 | +10.2 |
| | | **US Total** | **17 149** | | **20 012** | | |
| 784 | Auto parts and accessories | Mexico | 4 639 | 16.3 | 7 859 | 18.6 | +2.3 |
| | | China | 440 | 1.5 | 1 993 | 4.7 | +3.2 |
| | | **US Total** | **28 440** | | **42 255** | | |
| 821 | Furniture | Mexico | 3 202 | 16.9 | 4 297 | 14.0 | –2.9 |
| | | China | 4 476 | 23.6 | 13 187 | 43.0 | +19.4 |
| | | **US Total** | **18 927** | | **30 636** | | |
| 84 | Articles of apparel and clothing | Mexico | 8 731 | 13.6 | 6 322 | 8.3 | –5.3 |
| | | China | 8 483 | 13.2 | 19 931 | 26.1 | +12.9 |
| | | **US Total** | **64 296** | | **76 380** | | |

Source: US International Trade Commission (http://dataweb.usitc.gov, downloaded on 3 March, 2006.

However, if we increase the threshold to 40 per cent or more of US imports, Mexico had three such products and China had 13. For example, more than two-thirds of all footwear imported to the United States comes from China, while China also accounts for over 55 per cent of US imports of clothes and television or sound recorders (DVDs) and nearly 50 per cent of imported office machines, automatic data processing machines, and household appliances.

Why has China gained US market share over Mexico so rapidly and decisively? There are several factors. First, China has significantly lower labour costs than Mexico. In 2002, the US Bureau of Labor Statistics calculated

**Table 2.5. Select US imports in which Mexico and/or China hold 20 per cent or more of the US market, 2005**

| Product | (SITC categories) | % Market Share in USA | Change in % Market Share 2000-05 |
|---|---|---|---|
| **Mexico** | | | |
| 054 | Vegetables, fresh, chilled, frozen; roots, tubers and other edible vegs | 60.6 | −0.4 |
| 773 | Equipement for distributing electricity, n.e.s. | 57.5 | −3.2 |
| 761 | TV receivers (including video monitors & projectors) | 45.6 | −17.9 |
| 782 | Motor vehicles for the transport of goods | 37.3 | 5.7 |
| 772 | Electrical apparatus for swithing of portecting electrical circuits | 28.0 | 3.5 |
| 716 | Rotating electric plant and parts thereof n.e.s. | 27.9 | −5.0 |
| 778 | Electrical machinery and apparatus n.e.s. | 21.8 | 3.5 |
| 872 | Instruments and appliances for medical, surgical, dental or veterinary purposes | 21.7 | 1.5 |
| 713 | Internal combustion piston engines and part thereof, n.e.s. | 20.3 | 3.3 |
| 775 | Household type electrical and nonelectrical equipment | 20.0 | 0.4 |
| **China** | | | |
| 894 | Baby carriages, toys, games and sporting goods | 78.0 | 13.5 |
| 831 | Trunks, suitcases, vanity cases, binocular, camera cases, handbags, wallets, etc. | 73.8 | 24.0 |
| 851 | Footwear | 70.9 | 9.0 |
| 813 | Lighting fixtures and fittings, n.e.s. | 65.1 | 6.8 |
| 697 | Household equipment of base metal, n.e.s. | 57.6 | 22.0 |
| 763 | Sound recorders; television image and sound recorders | 57.1 | 34.9 |
| 848 | Articles of apparel and clothing accessories; nontextile fabrics | 56.0 | 11.2 |
| 751 | Office machines | 49.0 | 19.9 |
| 752 | Automatic data processing machines; magnetic or optical readers | 47.1 | 35.8 |
| 775 | Household type electrical and nonelectrical equip. | 46.8 | 9.6 |
| 658 | Made-up articles of textile | 43.9 | 19.8 |

**Table 2.5. (cont.)**

| Product | (SITC categories) | % Market Share in USA | Change in % Market Share 2000-05 |
|---|---|---|---|
| 821 | Furniture and parts; bedding, mettresses, supports, cushions | 43.0 | 19.4 |
| 762 | Radio-broadcast receivers | 41.1 | 5.7 |
| 893 | Articles, n.e.s. of plastics | 38.3 | 7.5 |
| 899 | Miscellaneous manufactured articles | 34.4 | −8.3 |
| 759 | Parts and accessories for use office machines | 33.2 | 21.7 |
| 771 | Electric power machinery | 32.9 | 11.1 |
| 842 | Women's or girls' coats, capes, jackets, suits, trousers, dresses, skirts, underwear, etc. of woven | 32.0 | 16.2 |
| 764 | Telecommunications equipment, n.e.s. and telecommunications accessories | 28.9 | 18.6 |
| 699 | Manufactures of base metal, n.e.s. | 26.3 | 12.7 |
| 845 | Articles of apparel, of textile fabrics, whether or not knitted or crocheted | 24.1 | 13.2 |
| 761 | TV receivers (including video monitors & projectors) | 23.1 | 20.6 |
| 778 | Electrical machinery and apparatus | 22.1 | 10.2 |
| 897 | Jewelry goldsmiths' and silversmiths' wares, and other articles of precious or semiprecious materials | 20.8 | 11.0 |

Product selection criteria: Over $2 billion in US Imports from China or Mexico in 2005 at the 3-digit SITC level

Source: U.S. International Trade Commission (http://dataweb.usitc.gov), downloaded on April 14, 2006.

China's average manufacturing compensation at $0.64 an hour,[21] compared with Mexico's US$2.48 (*Business Week*, 2004). It remains to be seen if this gap will widen, shrink, or be maintained in coming years. Persistent labour shortages are now being reported at hundreds of Chinese factories, a trend that is pushing up wages and leading a number of manufacturers to consider moving their factories to lower-cost countries like Vietnam (Barboza, 2006; Goodman, 2005).

Second, China has sought to leverage its huge economies of scale, and it has made major investments in infrastructure and logistics to lower transportation costs and to speed time to market for export products. The growth of China's "supply-chain cities" – led by foreign investor-driven clusters in

---

[21] China's 30 million city manufacturing workers on whom data could be found earned an average of US$1.06 an hour, while 71 million suburban and rural manufacturing workers earned 45 cents an hour, for a blended average of 64 cents (*Business Week*, 2004).

Guangdong (including Dongguan and Humen) and single-product clusters in Zhejiang (such as Anji and Datang) – is a perfect illustration of how China's governments and entrepreneurs are turning scale-driven specialization into a persistent competitive advantage for the country (Wang and Tong, 2002; Zhang et al., 2004; Sonobe et al., 2002).

Third, China has a coherent and multidimensional upgrading strategy to diversify its industrial mix and to add high-value activities. In their careful study of China's export performance, Lall and Albaladejo (2004) argue that China and its East Asian neighbours are developing high-technology exports in a regionally integrated fashion, based on complex networks of export production that link leading electronics multinationals and their first-tier suppliers and global contract manufacturers (see also Sturgeon and Lee, 2005; Gereffi et al., 2005; Gereffi, 1996). The export patterns for high-tech products reveal complementarity rather than confrontation between China and its mature East Asian partners (Japan, Republic of Korea, Taiwan (China), and Singapore). China's role as a motor of export growth for the region, however, could change as China itself moves up the value chain and takes over activities currently carried out by its regional neighbours. Rodrik (2006) suggests that China is already exporting a wide range of highly sophisticated products, and he calculates that China's export bundle is similar to that of a country whose per capita income is three times higher than China's current level.

Fourth, China is using foreign direct investment to promote "fast learning" in new industries and knowledge spillovers in its domestic market (Zhang and Felmingham, 2002; Wang and Meng, 2004). Despite restrictions imposed by the WTO against domestic performance requirements for foreign firms, China's local market is sufficiently attractive for multinational manufacturers that they are willing to comply with the wishes of local, regional and national government authorities, despite stringent technology transfer requirements.

## A note on China's supply chain cities and industrial upgrading[22]

The concept of "supply chain cities" has been used in media reports and academic literature to highlight the growth of large-scale production in China and the agglomeration of multiple stages of the value chain in particular locales within China as a key to its upgrading success. Barboza (2004), for example, lays out the incredible specialization and scale that characterizes China's diversified export success in the apparel industry, even before the phase-out of the Multifibre Arrangement and apparel quotas by the WTO on 1 January 2005.

---

[22]  The research and editorial assistance of Ryan Ong in preparing this section is gratefully acknowledged.

The term "supply-chain cities" encompasses two distinct, but related, phenomena in China. The first usage refers to giant, vertically-integrated *firm factories*. Appelbaum (2005), as well as a variety of textile journals and large textile/apparel companies like Luen Thai (2004), use "supply chain city" to indicate a new breed of "super-factory" that firms are constructing in China and in other parts of Asia (Kahn, 2004; Pang, 2004). These factories are company-specific, and are designed to bring together multiple parts of the firm's supply chain – designers, suppliers, and manufacturers – so as to minimize transaction costs, take advantage of economies of scale, and foster more flexible supply chain management. Luen Thai's factories in Guangdong Province (in Dongguan, Qingyuan, and Panyu) are exemplars of this approach. [23] Many of the firms actively establishing these giant factories are from Hong Kong and Taiwan.

A second usage of this term refers to so-called *cluster cities*. Barboza (2004) and others use "supply chain cities" when discussing the growing number of single-product industrial clusters that have sprung up in China's coastal regions. These areas have dramatically increased production of one specific product, and are churning out massive volume, but are not limited to manufacturing firms. As these clusters have grown, they have attracted related and supporting businesses, including yarn dealers, sewers, pressers, packagers, and freight forwarders. These clusters also feature large sprawling factories, with factory buildings, dormitories, and limited amenities for workers, but the focus here is on the overall cluster of firms. Illustrative examples include Datang (socks) and Shengzhou (neckties) (see Wang and Tong, 2002; Wang et al., 2005; Kusterbeck, 2005; Zhang et al., 2004).

What forces drive the formation of China's supply-chain cities? In addressing this question, bottom-up versus top-down metaphors offer a misleading dichotomy for China, simply because both characterizations are oversimplified. "Top-down" implies that development patterns are directed closely by the central government, while "bottom-up" implies that development patterns are determined purely by market forces. The reality in China lies somewhere in the middle.

(a)  "Supply-chain city" super-factories appear to be more bottom-up than top-down, since they result from individual sourcing decisions by private firms and are not directed by central government policy. The location of many of these factories is tied to existing manufacturing activities and the low cost of factor inputs (land, electricity, labour), though local and provincial govern-

---

[23]  In Dongguan, in southern China, apparel maker Luen Thai Holdings Ltd. boasts of a "supply-chain city" that is a two-million square foot facility that includes a factory, dormitories for 4,000 workers, and a 300-room hotel (Kahn, 2004). Appelbaum (2005, pp. 7-8) describes Hong Kong-based Yue Yuen - the world's largest footwear supplier - as a company that made nearly 160 million pairs of shoes for export in 2003, one-sixth of the world total of branded athletic and casual footwear. One of its four Dongguan factories employs as many as 70,000 workers.

Figure 2.3. China's supply chain cities in apparel

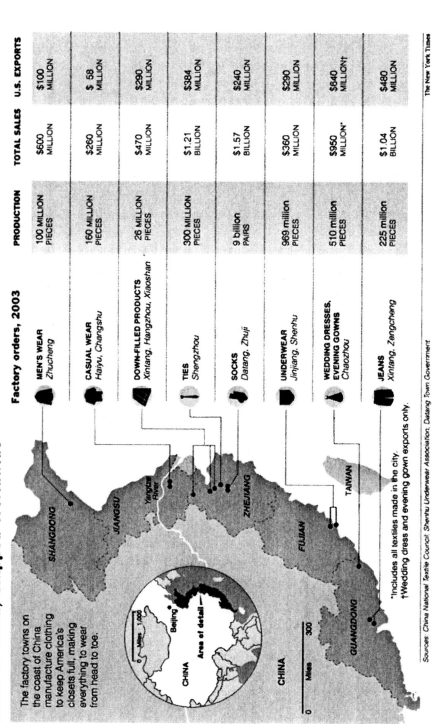

## Made in China, Shipped Worldwide

The factory towns on the coast of China manufacture clothing to keep America's closets full, making everything to wear from head to toe.

| Factory orders, 2003 | PRODUCTION | TOTAL SALES | U.S. EXPORTS |
|---|---|---|---|
| MEN'S WEAR Zhucheng | 100 MILLION PIECES | $600 MILLION | $100 MILLION |
| CASUAL WEAR Haiyu, Changshu | 160 MILLION PIECES | $260 MILLION | $ 58 MILLION |
| DOWN-FILLED PRODUCTS Xintang, Hangzhou, Xiaoshan | 26 MILLION PIECES | $470 MILLION | $290 MILLION |
| TIES Shengzhou | 300 MILLION PIECES | $1.21 BILLION | $384 MILLION |
| SOCKS Datang, Zhuji | 9 billion PAIRS | $1.57 BILLION | $240 MILLION |
| UNDERWEAR Jinjiang, Shenhu | 969 million PIECES | $360 MILLION | $290 MILLION |
| WEDDING DRESSES, EVENING GOWNS Chaozhou | 510 million PIECES | $950 MILLION* | $640 MILLION† |
| JEANS Xintang, Zengcheng | 225 million PIECES | $1.04 BILLION | $480 MILLION |

*Includes all textiles made in the city.
†Wedding dress and evening gown exports only.

Sources: China National Textile Council; Shenhu Underwear Association; Datang Town Government

The New York Times

Source: David Barboza, "In roaring China, sweaters are west of socks city", *New York Times*, Dec. 24, 2004.

35

ment has played a key role in providing a beneficial policy environment (tax incentives, streamlining bureaucratic red tape, etc.)

(b)   As for the formation of clusters, this story is more complicated, and involves regional, technological, and industry factors. There is a growing body of scholarship – mainly in Chinese – on this topic, addressing the economic, policy, cultural, and historical reasons behind cluster formation.[24] At the risk of overgeneralizing China's current situation, the major analytical divide in these clusters seems to be between clusters whose formation was driven initially by foreign capital, and those whose formation was initiated by domestic entrepreneurship.

The *foreign-led clusters* were founded first in the 1970s and 1980s as export-oriented production platforms, mainly in South China (Guangdong, Fujian). These began in low-cost manufacturing industries, including textiles and apparel, and have now expanded to include newer industries like electronics. Foreign investment was particularly important, with large investments coming from Hong Kong, Taiwan, and Macao; thus the central government's role in determining the policy environment for foreign investors was important. These clusters were founded in South China due to its low-cost labour and its relative proximity to both investors and major transportation Centres. Guangdong (close to Hong Kong) and Fujian (across from Taiwan) were pioneers of this type of cluster, with larger cities in the Yangtze River Delta (Shaoxing, Hangzhou) developing at a later date (see Zhang et al., 2004; Wang and Tong, 2002).

The *Chinese-led clusters* are mainly in Zhejiang and Jiangsu provinces (near Shanghai), and began to grow more rapidly in the 1990s. These clusters are based on so-called town and village enterprises that were a major part of the government's push for economic development in the 1980s and 1990s, and are often in traditionally rural areas. In Zhejiang, many of these clusters were founded by chance – with a confluence of historical knowledge, individual entrepreneurship, networking, and pure luck – but continued to grow because of conscious local government policy. Thus, private entrepreneurship is critical, but the government had an important facilitative role (Wang et al., 2005, p. 12; Zhang et al., 2004, pp. 7-8; Sonobe et al., 2002).

An additional question is whether these clusters are seeking to upgrade and move up the value chain. Again, it is helpful to separate our clusters into two groups.

- *South China:* The foreign-led cluster cities in Guangdong and Fujian seem to be further along in terms of fostering new, higher-tech industries, building firms with international brands, and featuring a broader

---

[24]   My appreciation goes to Ryan Ong for his insights on this literature.

export mix in traditional industries. The growth of the electronics industry is a good example (Lüthje, 2004).

- *East China:* These cities lie at an earlier point on the development trajectory, and Chinese authors such as Jici Wang have commented that these areas are still producing at the low-end of the technology value chain. Even here, firms and government officials are increasingly conscious of their need to find new competitive advantages, especially in the face of rising labour costs and growing competition from other locations (Wang and Tong, 2002; Wang et al., 2005).

## Shifting development strategies and regional linkages

Both China and Mexico currently face a host of new social and economic problems – corruption, environmental degradation, income inequality – and they are actively questioning the merits of a neoliberal, export-led growth model (Nolan, 2005). Each nation faces criticism that previous paradigms of development have left parts of the economy vulnerable to foreign control or foreign pressure. In each case, reformers are calling for new social welfare programmes to address their concerns, and they confront those who argue that only a fuller implementation of neoliberalism can address the problems of development.

China's growing economic links with Mexico and Latin America also make this comparison a valuable one. Latin America has become an important source of raw material exports to China in the last decade, and a foreign policy priority as well, marked by major visits to the region by President Hu Jintao and Vice President Zeng Qinghong in the past two years. In addition, Mexico and China are competing for US markets in a widening array of product lines, ranging from textiles/apparel and furniture, to automotive and electronic products.

To understand China's development model and industrial upgrading experience, it is essential to situate China within emerging intra-regional trade and production networks in East Asia, as well as to examine China's broader role in the global economy. Foreign direct investment has facilitated China's export diversification, but China is also pioneering new forms of domestic industrial organization in the form of supply-chain cities. The Chinese model is predicated on a clear value-chain strategy of giving high-value activities the most attention, and thus there is a growing emphasis on research and development, design, science and engineering education, and brands.

This is a very difficult upgrading model for other countries to emulate, and China's future success is not guaranteed. Smaller economies in particular need to focus on developing specialized niches in global value chains in order to compete with much larger economies in both the developed and the developing world. China, India and Mexico are instructive cases because they have a lot of experience with upgrading in global markets. But other dimensions that are important to the ability of globalization to spread its benefits broadly and fairly are the public and private governance mechanisms that regulate the global economy, a subject to which we turn in the next lecture.

# Lecture 3.   Globalization and the demand for governance
*(co-authored by Gary Gereffi and Frederick Mayer)*

## The challenge to globalization

Halfway through the first decade of the twenty-first century, economic globalization continues to pose challenges for developing and developed countries alike. In the developing world, globalization has brought greater prosperity to some, but it has also left many other countries, sub-national regions, and individuals behind. Much of Africa and parts of Latin America and Asia have benefited little. Some initial beneficiaries of globalization, such as Mexico and Eastern Europe, are beginning to suffer competition from East Asia, and above all China. And even the biggest apparent winners, notably China and India, face strains in coping with the rapid changes that globalization has caused.

Globalization is not only a problem for developing countries. Although many in the advanced industries have benefited, traditional manufacturing heartlands across North America and Western Europe have declined in the face of competition from developing countries. Now, too, there are concerns about the loss of white-collar jobs to developing countries, as well-educated and highly paid workers are finding themselves traveling the same road their blue-collar peers took in the 1970s and 1980s. Both are suffering from "the triple threat of computerization, tech-led productivity gains, and the relocation of their jobs to offshore sites" (Schwartz, 2003). US-trained Indian radiologists in Bangalore can analyse CT scans and chest X-rays for less than half what would be paid to their counterparts in the United States, and Ernst & Young employs 200 accountants in India processing US tax returns (Schumer and Roberts, 2004).

These stresses reflect two dramatic changes in the structure of the global economy. The first is an historic shift in the location of production, particularly in manufacturing, from the developed to the developing world. As more and more countries have acquired the ability to make complex as well as standard manufactured goods, barriers to entry have fallen and competitive pressures in the production stage of global value chains have increased. The emergence of China, India, and other large developing nations has expanded the global labour force so significantly that a likely consequence of globalization is to bid down the living standards not only for unskilled work and primary products, but increasingly for skilled work and industrial products as well (Polaski, 2004; Kaplinsky, 2005).

The second is a change in the organization of the international economy. The global economy is increasingly concentrated at the top and fragmented at the bottom, both in terms of countries and firms. Because of this structure, profits are driven down at the base of global value chains because of intense competition, and there is no money for reinvestment, innovation, or for improving wages and profits among smaller producers. Developed and developing economies alike are now competing to capture the relatively high-value activities in global production networks.

As the report of the World Commission on the Social Dimensions of Globalization has put it, "The current process of globalization is generating unbalanced outcomes, both between and within countries. ... Meanwhile the revolution in global communications heightens awareness of these disparities" (ILO, 2004, p. x). These shifts reveal a sobering globalization paradox: the dramatic expansion of production capabilities reflected in global outsourcing across a wide range of industries does not necessarily increase sustainable development, generate adequate numbers of jobs, or contribute to poverty reduction in the exporting nations.

The economic and social stresses attributable to globalization have sparked resistance to the policies that promote it. In the developing world, particularly in Latin America and Africa, there is a growing rejection of free market and other neoliberal prescriptions and a desire for a return to a more managed economic system. Many developing countries complain that they lack the influence they deserve at the IMF, the WTO, and other global institutions where the rules are negotiated. In the advanced economies, a political backlash against outsourcing, particularly to China and India, appears to be brewing. And in the networks of labour, environmental, human rights, religious, and other activists that constitute an increasingly global civil society, there are protests against the social consequences of the new global economy.

The social response to globalization is often interpreted as merely a backlash against economic globalization. But much of the political activity around the globe is actually focused on something quite different. It is not so much a rejection of globalization as it is a demand for greater and more effective governance. As the report of the Commission on the Social Dimensions of

Globalization put it, the problem is that "Global markets have grown rapidly without the parallel development of economic and social institutions necessary for their smooth and equitable functioning" (ILO, 2004, p. xi). The response to globalization reflects a growing awareness that the new global economy has outstripped the existing capacities of governments, international institutions, and citizens to govern in ways that advance the interests and values of individuals, communities and nations.

In this lecture, we develop a broad framework for understanding the relationships between economic globalization, social response, and demands for new forms of governance. We argue that globalization has led to governance deficits that pose a threat to the stability of the global economy. However, as we discuss below, developments in three realms of governance – the thickening of international institutions, the emergence of a private form of governance involving interactions between civil society and corporations, and capacity building in developing countries – may allow the international system to adapt sufficiently to govern the global market. The question is whether it can adapt quickly enough.

## The nature of market governance

Before turning to the question of how globalization has created a governance deficit, it is useful to be clear about what we mean by market governance and how governance systems relate to markets. By *market governance* we mean those institutions, governmental and non-governmental, that both enable and constrain the behaviour of markets and market actors. We distinguish it from two other forms of governance: *corporate governance*, which deals with issues of accountability of firms to shareholders and employees; and *industrial governance*, which relates to the management of supply chains and inter-firm relationships.[25] Henceforward, when we refer to governance we mean governance of the market by non-market institutions of the state or society.

Governance is not the same thing as government. Governance systems may be public, i.e. governmental, but private governance can be equally or more important. Public governance is the familiar stuff of governmental policy: laws, regulations, enforcement capacities, and the like. Private governance involves non-governmental institutions in society and includes social mores that determine acceptable market behaviour, professional standards and codes of conduct, collective bargaining agreements that define the obligations of firms towards workers, and other societal conventions.

---

[25] For a discussion of the governance of global value chains, see Gereffi et al. (2005).

It is useful to conceive of governance in terms of different functions. Governance systems play at least three roles with respect to markets:

- *Facilitative* – Governance institutions play a crucial role in facilitating the operation of markets by establishing property rights, enforcing contracts, establishing rules of fair competition, providing information, and much more. No market, even the most primitive, can operate without some institutional context.

- *Regulatory* – Governance institutions are necessary to regulate the negative externalities of private market transactions. Without constraints (or incentives), markets would exploit and endanger workers, pollute the environment and over-harvest natural resources, and generate other negative externalities.

- *Distributive* – Governance institutions play a crucial role in limiting and mitigating the unequal impacts of markets and enabling societies to adjust to economic change. Distributive mechanisms include social insurance, health care, public education and retraining, progressive tax systems, and other welfare policies, all of which serve to temper the tendency of markets towards highly unequal outcomes.

Table 3.1 provides examples of each mode of governance.

**Table 3.1. A taxonomy of market governance**

| Modes of governance | Public | Private |
|---|---|---|
| Facilitative | Property rights; Banking and commercial policy; Competition policy. | Industry standards; Professional norms and codes. |
| Regulatory | Labour law; Environmental regulations; Health and safety regulations. | Corporate social responsibility; Codes of conduct; Green labelling. |
| Distributive | Social insurance; Public health and education; Progressive taxation. Philanthropy. | Collective bargaining; |

Figure 3.1 provides a highly stylized depiction of the relationship between market, state, and society in the modern welfare state. Here the market (firms, networks, and markets) is governed by both governmental and societal institutions, as denoted by the thick arrows labelled respectively *public governance* and *private governance*. There is, of course, considerable variation among the advanced industrial countries with respect to these arrangements,

Figure 3.1. Public and private governance in advanced industrial states

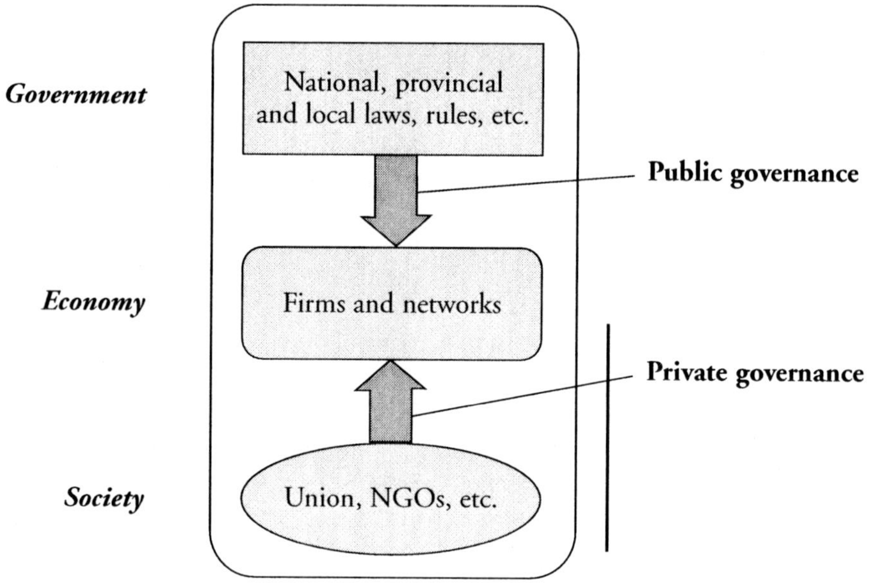

*Government*

*Economy*

*Society*

with some having a relatively larger role for the state and a lesser role for society, and some placing more emphasis on distributive governance than others.[26]

## Before globalization

In many ways, the current situation parallels that faced by industrializing nations in the first half of the twentieth century. As Polanyi argued, the rise of the modern industrial economy in the late nineteenth and early twentieth centuries created a relatively autonomous market that was no longer "embedded" in traditional institutions of government or community. This constituted a threat to workers, to nature, and even to the stability of markets themselves (Polanyi, 1944).

It was no accident that the welfare state developed with the rise of integrated national markets. The mature industrialized nations had developed thick systems of governance to facilitate the operation of markets, to regulate market actors, and to compensate for market effects. This co-existence of

---

[26]    We recognize that we are ignoring important differences among developed nations, as explored extensively in the varieties of capitalism literature (see, for example, Hall and Soskice, 2001; Kitschelt et al., 1999).

markets and governance, often contested, was crucial to the success of the modern industrial state. Without strong governance systems to facilitate market transactions, markets could not have prospered as they did. Without strong governance systems to regulate and distribute, societies would not long have tolerated free markets.

Historically, there was a rough congruence between the geography of markets and the scope of governance institutions. Both were, for the most part, organized on the unit of the nation-state. But as Polanyi writing in the early 1940s observed, the economic internationalization of the first decades of the twentieth century had created a market beyond national control, which was a major reason why it proved impossible to sustain. Polanyi predicted that there would be a retrenchment from international capitalism and a return to national markets as a means of restoring social control over markets.

Reviewing the post-war economy nearly 40 years later, John Ruggie judged that while Polanyi had been wrong in his prediction of the end of capitalist internationalism, he was essentially right in concluding that governments would need to assume a much greater role in providing a social safety net (Ruggie, 1982). In Ruggie's view, a system of "embedded liberalism" had enabled an increasingly open international economy by tying it to strong interventionist policies domestically and by retaining a measure of protection from international financial markets. After the Second World War, the Bretton Woods institutions, most notably the IMF and the General Agreement on Tariffs and Trade (GATT), helped to facilitate the growth of international commerce by providing greater stability, but markets and market governance remained predominantly national in scope, and regulatory and distributive functions of governance could be accomplished by national governance systems.

Figure 3.2 illustrates in highly stylized form the world before globalization as it emerged in the post-war era. In the developed world, the market is internationalized, with relatively low barriers to trade and investment. There exists a high degree of economic interdependence, which is facilitated at the international level by the Bretton Woods institutions (Keohane and Nye, 1977). But international regulatory organizations such as the International Labour Organization (ILO) are quite weak and the distributive capacity of the World Bank and others is highly limited. Market governance, therefore, is largely concentrated at the national level, where thick and roughly comparable systems of public and private governance constitute an implicit international social compact.

It is important to note, as Ruggie (1982) highlights, that this system of embedded liberalism operated only within the developed world among the advanced industrial states. The Soviet Union, Eastern and Central Europe, and China remained centrally planned economies playing by completely different rules; Latin America was largely enthralled by import substitution policies that

44

**Figure 3.2. Before globalization (pre 1980s): Embedded liberalism and limited internationalization**

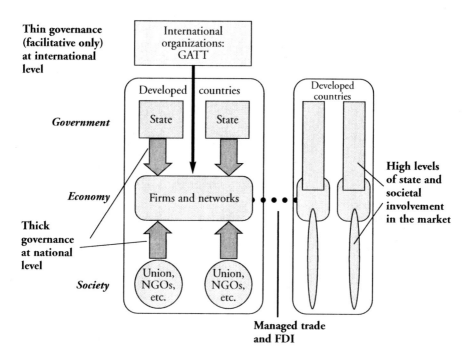

insulated it from world commerce; and Africa and India were still emerging from a pattern of colonial dependency. As depicted in figure 3.2, the developing world (here highly simplified) is to a significant degree outside the international market. Commerce between developed and developing countries is largely in the form of managed trade and limited direct foreign investment, particularly in extractive industries. Within the developed world, the relationship between state, market and society is much more intertwined, whether in the centrally planned economies or in more corporatist economies, with high levels of public ownership and other forms of market intervention and less independence for labour unions and other societal institutions. There are few of the regulatory and distributive mechanisms present in the advanced industrial countries.

## Globalization and governance deficits

In the quarter century since Ruggie wrote, processes of internationalization have altered the global landscape. The collapse of communism in Russia, Europe and China, the abandonment of import substitution for free market liberalism in Latin America and elsewhere (in part due to pressure from the IMF), and the series of multilateral trade negotiations that culminated in the WTO, transformed the policy environment. Market actors responded by becoming increasingly international, both in the form of transnational corporations (TNCs) and in a growing reliance on the outsourcing of production to firms in the developing world. The large, vertically integrated TNCs that predominated in the 1950s and 1960s began to spread their global reach, initially through international subsidiaries fostered by the import-substitution policies of many developing economies. In the 1980s, the shift to export-oriented development models in much of the developing world, coupled with the growth in the industrial capabilities of offshore suppliers, contributed to the vertical disintegration of TNCs, especially in consumer goods industries, and the rise of international production networks in which TNCs emphasized coordination and control over relatively high-value activities, rather than ownership (Dicken, 2003). As Milner (1988) has shown, the increasingly international outlook of corporations made them supportive of further market opening, thus reinforcing the process of internationalization.

Economic globalization has dramatically altered the international market of the post-war era in two significant ways. The first is a profound shift in the location of manufacturing production, and to a lesser but growing extent of services, from the developed to the developing world. Once largely outside the global production system, Brazil, China, India, Mexico and other smaller countries now constitute a huge and rapidly growing portion of it. By the end of the 1990s, around half of all manufacturing jobs were in developing countries, and 60 per cent of exports from developing countries to the industrialized world were manufactured goods (Held and McGrew, 2002, p. 3). Clearly, a very large proportion of global production is now outside the advanced industrial economies.

The second change is equally significant for governance. Whereas once international production was organized on a national scale with international commerce primarily a matter of arms-length trade and capital flows, the new global economy is increasingly characterized by production and supply networks that transcend national boundaries (Palmisano, 2006). As we noted earlier, in many industrial sectors this system is highly concentrated at the top of global value chains, with a limited number of branded firms controlling a highly fragmented and intensely competitive network of producers at the bottom of the value chain. A large proportion of international trade is now intra-firm or utilizes sophisticated inter-firm networks (Gereffi et al., 2005).

It is important to recognize the fundamental asymmetry in the organization of the global economy between more and less developed nations. To a great extent, the concentrated higher-value-added portion of the value chain is located in developed countries, while the lower-value-added portion of the value chain is in developing economies. Countries in the periphery of the global production system thus tend to have the most commodified, fragmented, and cost-driven portion of the production system. A similar pattern is apparent in agricultural production. Although it is true that there has long been a global production system in agriculture, today production is much more controlled by a limited number of TNCs located in the developed world.

In financial markets, the post-war Bretton Woods institutions of the IMF and the World Bank constituted strong facilitative and distributive capacity, respectively, for an international system largely reserved for the developed world. In the 1980s, the focus of those institutions shifted to bringing the developing world into the global financial system, but with little attention to the governance implications of such integration. Indeed, conditionality served to break apart old systems of national governance that involved high levels of protection, regulation, and state involvement, which whatever their failings did serve important regulatory and distributive functions. As Rodrik and others have demonstrated, the rapid integration of international financial markets, without adequate governance capacity at either the national or international level, has exposed developing countries to high levels of volatility and risk (Rodrik, 1997, 1999).

Governance systems have been slow to adapt. The consequence, we argue, is a mismatch between the global economy and the institutions of market governance. This mismatch has led to three governance deficits, as illustrated in figure 3.3.

The first governance deficit is the mismatch between the global economy and the governance institutions of advanced industrial states. As national borders have become increasingly porous and larger portions of the global economy are located in the developing world, the old governance structures, organized on the unit of the nation-state, have lost some of their capacity to effectively shape the market. One obvious implication is that much global production is simply beyond the reach of national institutions in the developed world. Although to date there appears no dramatic "race to the bottom," there is nonetheless good reason to believe that outsourcing and the threat of outsourcing has had a chilling effect on regulatory policy in the advanced industrial nations. Perhaps more important, however, has been the impact on distributive capacity. Intense global competition at the level of basic production, the wage and benefit gap between the developed and developing world, and the rapidity of economic change has put enormous pressure on both public and private governance institutions. In the public realm, social insurance, health care, and other elements of the social welfare state are unable to compensate those who lose out in the international marketplace. In the private realm, there is a clear erosion of the implicit social compact that long governed

**Figure 3.3. Globalization and governance deficits (mid 1980s to mid 1990s)**

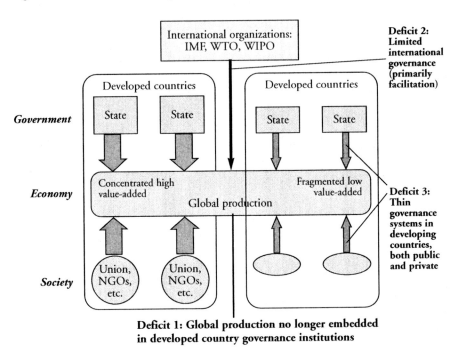

Deficit 1: Global production no longer embedded
in developed country governance institutions

business-labour relations and that included wage, pension, health, and other benefits. [27]

The second governance deficit is at the level of international organizations. Although international governance institutions such as the WTO, the IMF, and the World Intellectual Property Organization (WIPO) designed to facilitate global markets have continued to grow in strength, the development of regulatory and redistributive capacity at the global level has not kept pace. Intergovernmental organizations dealing with labour, the environment, and other social issues remain relatively weak. Certainly, in none of these realms is there anything approaching the binding and enforceable international standards of the WTO.

The third governance deficit is within developing countries, which have historically had very limited capacity to govern markets. In the heyday of

---

[27]     In this regard, as in others, the European Union is an exception to the general trend, but it also is an illustration of the broader point about the need to develop stronger international institutions. Europe has responded to the governance challenge posed by globalization by establishing a sizable internal market and by simultaneously developing thick governance institutions at the European level that have enabled it, so far, to maintain much of its regulatory and distributive apparatus.

neoliberalism, there was little understanding of the importance of governance in enabling a successful entry into the global economy. Most attention was focused on facilitative capacities: strengthening the rule of law, intellectual property rights, international standards, and the like. But whether they were making the transition from a non-market economy or from a relatively insulated corporatist model of governance, developing countries generally lacked the kind of robust regulatory and distributive institutions that characterized the advanced industrial nations. This is true both in the public and the private realm. In the public realm, few governments had anywhere near the regulatory capacity they need to monitor and enforce standards even where they exist, and public health, education, pension and other standard elements of the social safety net were grossly under-funded. In the private realm, the history of state dependency left most developing countries with little tradition of non-governmental organizations and other societal institutions. As a consequence, the rapid entry of many developing countries into the global economy made their old systems of governance obsolete and created a large governance deficit.

There are, of course, important differences within the developing world not reflected in our illustration. We can classify developing countries into at least four categories that reflect both their level of development and their relationship to the global economy. In the first category are the newly industrialized economies, which include the Republic of Korea, Singapore, Thailand, and Taiwan (China). In the second are the large emerging market economies, foremost among them China, India, Russia, Brazil, Indonesia and Mexico. In the third category are smaller developing countries that are closely connected to the international economy, including Central America, much of South America, most of Eastern Europe, and others such as Egypt, Vietnam, and Mauritius. Finally, there are those countries still largely outside the global economy, including most of sub-Saharan Africa.

## The governance response

In response to these governance deficits, forces in society have mobilized to demand new and more effective forms of governance. In this section, we explore the nature of the societal pressures arising from economic globalization. We argue that three seemingly unrelated developments – the push to "thicken" international governance by strengthening the regulatory and distributive capacity of international institutions, the rise of a global civil society pressing for corporate social responsibility, and the effort to build greater governance capacity in developing countries – constitute distinct responses to the same demand for governance.

## Social pressures and the demand for governance

In Polanyian terms, globalization and governance deficits have triggered a global social response. In part, the response can be billed as anti-globalization, a protest against institutions such as WTO that have facilitated the explosive growth of international trade, investment, and finance. But in part, the response is a demand for new forms of governance. As with all social movements, the social forces protesting aspects of globalization face significant collective action problems in mobilizing. Nonetheless, they have clearly succeeded in altering the political and intellectual climate for globalization, and created demands for governance that cannot be ignored.

The contemporary social response to globalization could be traced to many moments, but in the United States the controversy surrounding the North American Free Trade Agreement (NAFTA) was seminal. From the announcement in 1990 that the United States intended to seek a free trade agreement with Mexico, its less developed neighbour to the south, to the eventual passage in 1993 of NAFTA's implementing legislation by the US Congress, there arose a remarkably broad and intense opposition that almost scuttled the agreement (Mayer, 1998). Many of the concerns were specific to the spectre of an open border with Mexico, but there was also a more general sense of outrage that corporate-sponsored international liberalization was moving full steam ahead, while the regulatory concerns, social safety nets and adjustment assistance traditionally provided by national governments were endangered. For many, the historic compromise of embedded liberalism whereby economic liberalization was rooted in social community, characterized by the New Deal in the United States and social democracy in Europe, was being undone (Ruggie 2002a; 2002b).

In the past decade, the protest against globalization has gone global. The annual gathering of the World Social Forum, usually in Brazil, and the protests against the proposed Multilateral Investment Agreement in 1998, the WTO trade talks in Seattle in 1999, Cancún in 2003, and Hong Kong in 2005, and the vocal dissidents present at virtually every major economic summit of the last decade, all testify to the breadth and depth of the global network of protest. As markets have gone global, many in the developing world have sensed that globalization, whatever its benefits, also brings greater vulnerability to unfamiliar and unpredictable forces that can result in economic instability and social dislocation, as well as a flattening of local and national culture in the face of well-financed global marketing machines and "brand bullies" (Rodrik, 1997; Klein, 1999; Ritzer, 2000).

Although many aspects of economic globalization continue apace, political support for the simple prescriptions of free trade, privatization, and deregulation (the pillars of the "Washington consensus") has clearly waned. This is

**Figure 3.4. Three governance responses: 1990s to present**

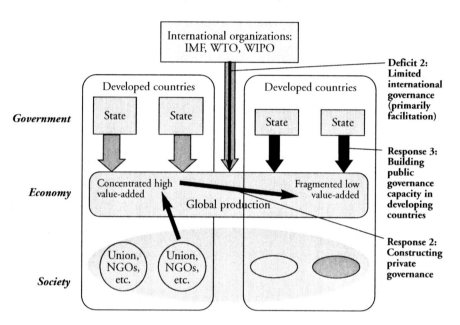

particularly obvious in Latin America, where the elections of Lula in Brazil, Chavez in Venezuela, and most recently Evo Morales in Bolivia, represent in part a protest against what might be called a "facilitation only" approach to market governance. Demands for "policy space" are high on the list of developing countries as they negotiate at the WTO in Geneva and seek to maintain their ability to manage the economic forces of market openness. And in Europe and North America, political resistance by agriculture, textile workers, and others has translated into a "go slow" approach to market opening.

Some have predicted that globalization will likely lead to its own demise, as an increasingly ungovernable and unaccountable global market triggers such a crisis that contemporary globalization will meet the same fate as economic internationalization during the first half of the twentieth century. In the absence of a global government and a true global polity, there are no governance institutions with the capacity to provide the regulatory and distributive functions necessary to sustain the market.[28]

But there is another possibility, one in which new institutions arise to fill the governance deficits. Seeds of that development are evident in three arenas of governance, as illustrated in figure 3.4. The first is the "thickening" of institutions at the international level, the second the possibility of building

---

[28] For a particularly wry version of this line of thinking, see *The Lugano Report* by George (2003).

a system of private governance in the interaction between civil society and corporations, and the third is in building governance capacity in developing countries.

## Thickening international institutions

One response to the governance deficit is the push to strengthen governance capacity at the international level. Over the last few decades, this demand has translated into pressures for stronger international rules dealing with everything from child labour to climate change, and for a much stronger development agenda to help poorer countries share in the benefits of globalization. Societal actors have attempted to link social concerns to the market-opening agenda. This push is most advanced at the regional level, especially in Europe, where continental economic integration has been accompanied by the creation of strong regulatory, social, and development institutions. Whether other regions of the world will be able to emulate the European model, and indeed whether that model is sustainable in the face of global competition, remains an open question.

In North America, NAFTA, unlike the European Union, was initially envisioned as purely a free trade (and investment) agreement, with few provisions to deal with the governance implications of integrating a developing economy (Mexico) with two advanced industrial ones (the United States and Canada). From the outset, NAFTA was a highly contentious issue in US politics. Organized labour immediately saw it as one more step down the path of corporate outsourcing, in which US workers were increasingly forced to compete with low-wage labour in other countries. Environmentalists saw free trade with Mexico as opening the door for polluting companies to move to Mexico. Both groups also saw NAFTA as a force for deregulation at the national level. In 1993, to obtain sufficient Congressional support to pass the NAFTA implementing bill in the face of this societal resistance in the United States, the Clinton Administration compelled Mexico to negotiate separate labour and environmental "side agreements," intended to ensure that there would be no "race to the bottom" with Mexico (Mayer, 1998).

Few social activists were satisfied with what was accomplished in the context of NAFTA, but labour and environmental groups have pursued this logic of linkage in subsequent US free trade negotiations. In both the US-Jordan and US-Cambodian Free Trade Agreements, which entered into effect in December 2001, as well as the US free trade agreements later negotiated with Chile and Singapore, some labour and environmental provisions were moved from side agreements into the main text of the trade accords. The US-Cambodia agreement is considered particularly important because the International Labour Organization agreed to undertake a monitoring programme in the textile and apparel sector, to report its results in a credible, efficient and transparent manner, and to make quota levels contingent on adequate performance (ILO, 2002).

Nevertheless, the prospects for further progress on the "trade-plus" front seem limited. Advocates for worker rights had hoped for strong linkage in the context of the US-Central American Free Trade Agreement (CAFTA), but in the end the agreement was negotiated and implemented without such provisions. Similarly, it is highly unlikely that the Free Trade Agreement of the Americas (FTAA), even if it were revived (currently a very dim prospect), would include significant new institutions for dealing with labour, environmental, or other social impacts of free trade. In the multilateral WTO negotiations, the Clinton Administration had been pushing for environmental and labour linkages in the Doha Round, but the effort was doomed by strong resistance from developing countries, which perhaps rightly feared that making free trade conditional on regulatory performance would leave them vulnerable to political forces they couldn't control as well as to the indifference of the Bush Administration to regulatory matters.

Rhetorically, at least, the current multilateral WTO negotiations were to be the "development round," which developing countries took as an implicit promise of provisions that would aid them in coping with economic globalization. Foremost on the developing country agenda was the desire to force open developed country markets for agricultural products and other goods that remain highly protected, and there was also hope for more systematic efforts to link development policies to the trade agenda. It is now clear that if the talks are concluded, still far from a certainty, the agreement will not be accompanied by significant distributive measures, but will largely be a market facilitation exercise.

Outside of the WTO process, there are numerous other initiatives intended to strengthen international labour, environment, health, and development institutions. These efforts have met with some success, but they have not yet translated into institutions with anywhere near the strength of the WTO. Although there is a policy logic to thickening international governance capacity, there also appear to be significant limits to how far the dominant members of the international community are willing to go in this direction.

## Strengthening private governance: Corporate social responsibility, codes of conduct and certification

A different approach to addressing labour and environmental issues has emerged in the private governance arena from the confluence of interests among civil society and corporate actors. This "NGO-industrial complex" may have significant promise as a governance strategy (Gereffi et al., 2001).

In the textile and apparel sector, for example, aggressive campaigns by labour groups, non-governmental organizations (NGO)s, and student activists compelled apparel manufacturers to adopt stringent codes of conduct and establish independent monitoring. The revelation in 1995 of the virtual enslavement of Thai workers in a garment factory in El Monte, California, prompted the Clinton Administration to form a task force called the Apparel Industry Partnership (AIP). Composed of manufacturers, NGOs, unions, and US Labor Department representatives, the AIP forged a code of conduct for apparel firms, stipulating the payment of the local minimum or prevailing wage, that workers be at least 14 years old, and that workers not be required to work more than 60 hours per week (although they could work unlimited voluntary hours). In November 1998, the AIP created the Fair Labor Association as the monitoring organization that would implement this code of conduct. Subsequently, there has been a proliferation of different codes of conduct and factory monitoring systems in the apparel industry (Maquila Solidarity Network, 2002; Esbenshade, 2004).

More generally, a variety of new "private governance" certification institutions are emerging (Gereffi et al., 2001). These include: individual corporate codes of conduct; sectoral certification schemes involving NGOs, firms, labour, and other industry stakeholders; and third-party auditing systems, such as SA8000 for labour standards or the Forest Stewardship Council certification for sustainable forestry practices. The United Nations' Global Compact is an initiative that encourages the private sector to work with the United Nations, in partnership with international labour and civil society organizations, to move toward "good practices" in human rights, labour standards, and environmental sustainability in the global public domain. While sceptics claim there is little evidence to show that these codes have significant impact on corporate behaviour (Hilowitz, 1996; Seidman, 2003), proponents generally argue that new systems of certification, enforced either by global consumers or by institutional actors such as the United Nations, could provide the basis for improved regulatory frameworks (Fung et al., 2001; Williams, 2000).

The goal of private governance campaigns is to force the peak or lead firms in global supply chains to set higher standards of corporate conduct that lesser known suppliers would be forced to adopt (hence the arrows from TNCs to other developing country suppliers in figure 3.4). Brand-named multinational manufacturers (Levi Strauss, Nestle), retailers (Gap, Benetton), and marketers (companies like Nike, Liz Claiborne, and Disney) are the targets for campaigns by transnational NGO activists and labour groups usually based in developed countries that are intended to improve labour, environmental, and development conditions in Third World production locations. The logic of the private governance model is to identify the most profitable and visible branded companies at the apex of global supply chains, not because the conditions of their suppliers are the worst in the world (actually, they are often relatively good), but rather because these companies have to protect their reputation with consumers. Their global brand names become a double-edged sword: they are a source of great market power, but they also make branded companies vulnerable to charges of exploitation that could harm their image among consumers.

Despite considerable progress, various challenges confront the codes of conduct regime. First, there is a "free rider" problem: only a handful of the most visible branded companies currently have codes, and they are receiving the brunt of the criticism from NGOs and unions even though their standards tend to be well above the industry norm. Thus, efforts to defend the collective reputation of apparel brands are concentrated among the most visible branded firms,[29] and the large retailers and unbranded manufacturers who account for most of the global outsourcing in the apparel industry are not held accountable by the public for the labour violations of their offshore contractors.[30] Second, there is much discussion regarding the possibility of consolidating codes of conduct, many of whose provisions are virtually identical, in order to avoid the time and expense of carrying out repetitive factory audits for similar codes.

Private governance approaches, such as corporate codes of conduct and more extensive factory monitoring, can help to improve labour market conditions in some factories and in some developing countries. However, the regime of voluntary codes now in place is extremely vulnerable. Unless more firms are brought into the system, there is a chance that what has been accomplished so far will unravel. In any case, private governance responses probably need to be integrated wherever possible with public efforts and legal institutions before sustainable social change is possible.

Private governance also raises important normative questions and issues of legitimacy. A governance regime dominated by corporations and NGOs is not likely to be representative of society as a whole. To the extent that this regime supplants the role of legitimate national governments, for example, as some in the developing world contend, there may be reasons to limit the reach of private governance. Second, and in related fashion, to the extent that the private governance regime is dominated by Northern-based NGOs and TNCs, as it largely is at present, it is unlikely to represent the domestic needs or interests of developing nations. At minimum, therefore, voices from the South need to be included more explicitly in private governance regimes.

---

[29] The Gap, the largest US clothing chain with more than 3,000 stores and an estimated 3,000 factories in 50 countries, promoted its corporate responsibility campaign with the publication of its 2003 "Social Responsibility Report" (Gap Inc., 2004). While Gap monitors found problems in many of its overseas suppliers, and revoked its stamp of approval from 136 factories in 2003, it took a big step toward making its anti-sweatshop policy more transparent, and thereby placed pressure on its branded and unbranded competitors alike to do the same thing.

[30] However, Wal-Mart, the world's biggest retailer, is receiving increasingly intense scrutiny from NGOs and organized labour alike. One of the most active pressure groups is Wal-Mart Watch <http://walmartwatch.com/>.

## Building governance capacity in developing countries

The third approach for dealing with the governance deficits spawned by globalization is to build governance capacity in developing countries. As we have noted, many developing countries were initially overwhelmed by economic globalization, and entry into the global economy was a shock. As Rodrik and others have made clear, making openness work requires more than eliminating barriers to commerce (Rodrik, 1999: Ruggie, 2002b). Equally important is governance.

Most attention has been directed at building facilitative capacity. This would include such basics as strengthening the rule of law, ensuring enforcement of contracts, promulgating accounting regulations, and enacting intellectual property protections. But increasingly, there is an awareness of the importance of regulatory and distributive capacity as well.

Throughout the developing world, there is growing interest in the sustainability of development. In many ways this effort involves collaboration among international organizations, civil society groups, governments, and enlightened business groups. Similarly, there is growing recognition of the crucial importance of distributive capacity to economic development. This, too, takes many forms, from developing social insurance programmes to greater investment in public education.

Notwithstanding the promising direction of efforts to build governance capacity within developing countries, there are many obstacles, foremost among them the lack of resources commensurate with the need. Many, perhaps most, governments in the developing world do not have environmental or labour ministries with the clout to effectively monitor and enforce basic regulations, and have even less capacity to provide social insurance or other distributive measures. In this regard, governance capacity might be viewed as a luxury good, which can only be afforded as societies develop economically. There is something to this, of course; greater wealth does enable developing countries to strengthen governance institutions. In this view, market facilitation comes first; regulation and distribution second. In our view, however, developing countries are likely to fare better if they are able to simultaneously build facilitative, regulatory and distributive capacities.

Indeed, the governance challenges noted above are daunting for all countries, both developed and developing. One area of potential optimism is the emergence of governance capabilities at both sub-national and regional levels. For the large emerging markets, such as China, India, and Brazil, the uneven impact of integration into the global market across sub-national regions may allow governance capacity to emerge at the provincial or even local level. For smaller economies, which are often part of a regional production network, such as the economies of South-east Asia or Central America and the Caribbean, it may be necessary to look to the regional level for governance solutions. It is quite possible, therefore, that we will see the emergence of a multi-level system of governance in the developing world: regional, national, and sub-national.

## Conclusion: Are we at a turning point?

The next decade is a defining period for the global economic system. As economic globalization deepens, the governance deficit will likely grow more acute. Deeper economic globalization will require greater governance capacity. The contrast between robust facilitative institutions of governance and the lagging regulatory and distributive institutions is stark. At the international level, there has been only modest movement to establish stronger environmental, labour, or other regulatory institutions (in the form of the "trade plus" and private governance initiatives discussed earlier), and even less action to provide distributive mechanisms for redressing unequal market impacts. The experiment in private governance, while promising, is limited and fragile. And in developing countries, the need for regulatory and distributive capacity will likely outpace the growth of that capacity.

The Washington Consensus that dominated thinking about economic development for most of the 1980s and 1990s is in retreat. It is now clear that laissez-faire policies are insufficient as a development strategy and that, as the new industrial policy literature demonstrates, removing barriers is not enough (Rodrik, 2004, 2006b; Sabel, 2005). In part, success depends on more sophisticated market facilitation in the form of "strategic collaboration between the private sector and the government" (Rodrik, 2004, p. 3). In part, too, successful economic development requires distributive mechanisms that temper tendencies towards grossly unequal outcomes and limit the economic risk faced by individuals. As Rodrik (1999) has shown, strong social safety nets and other adjustment mechanisms are correlated with economic growth. And to be sustainable, development also requires regulatory institutions that limit negative impacts on environment, health, safety, and other social goods. Exploiting workers or the environment is not a good long-term development strategy.

We are not advocating either a return to the discredited state-centric policies that dominated thinking about economic development in the 1960s and 1970s, or the imposition of European-style welfare states. Obviously, it is possible to go too far in attempting to correct market failures through public policy, which in the process could introduce governmental failures that are at least as great. What is needed is appropriate and smart governance, tailored to the realities faced by developed and developing economies and responsive to the interests of their societies.

We believe that the clamour over globalization is at heart a social response to a crisis of governance – that is, of the inadequacy of institutions not only to *facilitate* market growth and stability, but also to *regulate* markets and market actors, and to *compensate* for undesirable effects of market transactions. The rise of an increasingly global economy no longer firmly rooted in nation-states, and encompassing a large portion of the developing world, has led to a *governance deficit* of considerable magnitude and demand for greater governance.

The globalization of the early part of the twentieth century collapsed, in part, because of the incongruence between market structure and governance institutions. Some have predicted the same fate for contemporary globalization. However, the combination of governance responses in the international arena, in the relationship between private economic and non-economic actors, and, perhaps most importantly, in the developing world, at regional, national and sub-national levels, may evolve into an effective new system of global governance. Just as the international system that emerged after the Second World War proved Polanyi wrong, it may yet be possible to develop a "fair globalization" in which economic gains will be more broadly shared, and a more complete array of governance mechanisms will mediate market forces to the benefit of both developing and developed economies.

# References

Allen, M.: "Analysis: Increasing standards in the supply chain", in *Ethical Corporation*, 15 Oct. 2002.

Amiti, M.; Wei, S.-J.: *Fear of service outsourcing: Is it justified?*, IMF Working Paper WP/04/186 (Washington, DC, International Monetary Fund, 2004).

Appelbaum, R. P.: *The emergence of giant transnational contractors in East Asia: Emergent trends in global supply chains*, Paper presented at conference on Global Networks: Interdisciplinary Perspectives on Commodity Chains, Yale University, 13-14 May 2005.

Arrighi, G..; Silver, B.J.; Brewer, B.: "Industrial convergence, globalization, and the persistence of the north-south divide", in *Studies in Comparative International Development*, 2003, Vol. 38, No. 1, pp. 3-31.

Barboza, D.: "In roaring China, sweaters are west of sock city", in *New York Times*, 24 Dec. 2004.

—: "Labor shortage in China may lead to trade shift", in *New York Times*, 3 Apr. 2006.

Bronfenbrenner, K.; Luce, S.: *The changing nature of corporate global restructuring: The impact of production shifts on jobs in the US, China, and around the globe*, submitted to US-China Economic and Security Review Commission, 14 Oct. 2004.

*Business Week*: "Just how cheap is Chinese labor?", 2 Dec. 2004.

Chadwick, W., Jr.: "Global trends in the information technology outsourcing services market", in *Industry Trade and Technology Review*, USITC Office of Industries, 1-9 Nov. 2003.

Dicken, P.: *Global shift: Reshaping the global economic map in the 21st century*, 4th ed. (London, Sage, 2003).

Dolan, C.; Humphrey, J.: "Governance and trade in fresh vegetables: The impact of UK supermarkets on the African horticulture industry", in *Journal of Development Studies*, 2000, Vol. 37, No. 2, pp. 147-176.

Dussel Peters, E.: *Polarizing Mexico: The Impact of Liberalization Strategy* (Boulder, Lynne Rienner, 2000).

*Economist*: "The new jobs migration", 21 Feb. 2004a, p. 11.

—: "The great hollowing-out myth", 21 Feb. 2004b, pp. 27-29.

Engardio, P.; Bernstein, A; Kripalani, M.: "Is your job next?", in *Business Week*, 3 Feb. 2003, pp. 50-60.

Engardio, P.; Einhorn, B.: "Outsourcing innovation", in *Business Week*, 21 Mar. 2005, pp. 46-53.

Esbenshade, J.: *Monitoring sweatshops: Workers, consumers, and the global apparel industry* (Philadelphia, Pennsylvania, Temple University Press, 2004).

Farrell, D.; Laboissière, M.A.; Rosenfeld, J.: "Sizing the emerging global labour market", in *The McKinsey Quarterly*, 2005, No. 3.

Friedman, T. L.: *The world is flat: A brief history of the twenty-first century* (New York, Farrar, Strauss and Giroux, 2005).

Fuller, D. B.: "Moving along the electronics value chain: Taiwan in the global economy, in Berger, S.; Lester, R.K. (eds.): *Global Taiwan: Building competitive strengths in a new international economy* (Armonk, New York, Sharpe, 2005).

Fung, A.; O'Rourke, D.; Sabel, C.: "Realizing labor standards: How transparency, competition, and sanctions could improve working conditions worldwide", in *Boston Review*, 2001, Feb./Mar.

Gap Inc.: *Social responsibility report*, 2003, released 21 May 2004. http://www.gapinc.com/social_resp/social_resp.htm

George, S.: The Lugano report: On preserving capitalism in the twenty-first century (London, Pluto Press, 2003).

Gereffi, G.: "The organization of buyer-driven global commodity chains: How US retailers shape overseas production networks", in Gereffi, G.; Korzeniewicz, M. (eds.): Commodity chains and global capitalism (Westport, Connecticut, Praeger, 1994).

—: "Commodity chains and regional divisions of labor in East Asia", in Journal of Asian Business, 1996, Vol. 12, No. 1, pp. 75-112.

—: "International trade and industrial upgrading in the apparel commodity chain", in Journal of International Economics, 1999, Vol. 48, No. 1, pp. 37-70.

—: "The global economy: Organization, governance and development", in Smelser, N. J.; Swedberg, R. (eds.): The handbook of economic sociology, 2nd ed. (Princeton, New Jersey, Princeton University Press and Russell Sage Foundation, 2005), pp. 160-182.

—; Kaplinsky, R. (eds.): "The value of value chains: Spreading the gains from globalisation", Special issue of IDS Bulletin, 2001, Vol. 32, No. 3.

—; Memodovic, O.: The global apparel value chain: What prospects for upgrading by developing countries? (Vienna, UNIDO, Strategic Research and Economy Branch, 2003). http://www.soc.duke.edu/~ggere/web/UNIDO-Global%20Apparel_2003pdf

—; Garcia-Johnson, R.; Sasser, E.: "The NGO-industrial complex", in *Foreign Policy*, 2001, No. 125, pp. 56-65.

—; Humphrey, J.; Sturgeon, T.: "The governance of global value chains", in *Review of International Political Economy*, 2005, Vol. 12, No. 1, pp. 78-104.

Goodman, P. S.: "China ventures southward: In search of cheaper labor, firms invest in Vietnam", in *Washington Post*, 6 Dec. 2005.

—: Pan, P. P.: "Wal-Mart and China leading the race to the bottom", in *Washington Post*, 8 Feb. 2004.

Hall, P. A.; Soskice, D. (eds.): *Varieties of capitalism: The institutional foundations of comparative advantage* (New York, Oxford University Press, 2001).

Held, D.; McGrew, A. (eds.): *Governing globalization: Power, authority and global governance* (Cambridge, UK, Polity Press, 2002).

Hilowitz, J.: *Labelling child labor products: A preliminary study* (Geneva, ILO, 1996).

Huang, Y.; Khanna, T.: "Can India overtake China?", in *Foreign Policy*, 2003, July-Aug., pp. 74-81.

ILO: *Third synthesis report on the working conditions situation in Cambodia's garment sector*, Social Dialogue Sector, June 2002. http://www.ilo.org/public/english/dialogue/ifpdial/cambodia3.htm

—: *Employment and social policy in respect of export processing zones*, Committee on Employment and Social Policy, GB.286/ESP/3, Mar. 2003.

—: A fair globalization: Creating opportunities for all, Report of the World Commission on the Social Dimension of Globalization, 2004. http://www.ilo.org/public/english/fairglobalization/report/index.htm

Kahn, G.: "Making labels for less: Supply-chain city transforms far-flung apparel industry", in *Wall Street Journal Online*, 13 Aug. 2004.

Kaplinsky, R.: "Globalisation and unequalisation: What can be learned from value chain analysis?", in *Journal of Development Studies*, 2000, Vol. 37, No. 2, pp. 117-146.

—: *Globalization, inequality and poverty* (Cambridge, UK, Polity Press, 2005).

Karamouzis, F.: *A look at India for offshore sourcing options*, Gartner Research, AV-18-8057, 29 July 2003.

Keohane, R. O.: "Governance in a partially globalized world", in Held, D.; McGrew, A. (eds.): *Governing globalization: Power, authority and global governance* (Cambridge, UK, Polity Press, 2002), pp. 325-347.

—; Nye, J.: *Power and Interdependence* (Boston, Little, Brown, 1977).

Kitschelt, H.; Lange, P.; Marks, G.; Stephens, J.D.: (eds.): *Continuity and change in contemporary capitalism* (New York, Cambridge University Press, 1999).

Klein, N.: *No logo: Taking aim at the brand bullies* (New York, Picador, 2000).

Kusterbeck, S.: "China appeals to US buyers with 'supply chain cities'", in *Apparel Magazine*, 1 Aug. 2005.

Lall, S.: "The technological structure and performance of developing country manufactured exports, 1985-98", in *Oxford Development Studies*, 2000, Vol. 28, No. 3, pp. 337-369.

—; Albaladejo, M.: "China's competitive performance: A threat to East Asian manufactured exports?", in *World Development*, 2004, Vol. 32, No. 9, pp. 1441-1466.

Lora, E.; Pagés, C.; Panizza, U.; Stein, E.: *A decade of development thinking* (Washington, DC: Inter-American Development Bank, 2004).

Luen Thai: *Interim results 2004*, Corporate presentation (Luen Thai Holdings Limited, 2004).

Lüthje, B.: *Global production networks and industrial upgrading in China: The case of electronics contract manufacturing*, East-West Center Working Paper No. 74, 2004. http://www.eastwestcenter.org/stored/pdfs/ECONwp074.pdf

Maquila Solidarity Network: Memo: *Codes Update*, No. 17, Nov. 2002.

Mayer, F. W.: Interpreting *NAFTA: The science and art of political analysis* (New York, Columbia, 1998).

McKendrick, D.; Doner, R.F.; Haggard, S.: *From Silicon Valley to Singapore: Location and competitive advantage in the hard disk drive industry* (Stanford, California, Stanford University Press, 2000).

McKinsey Global Institute: *The emerging global labor market*, June 2005. http://www.mckinsey.com/mgi/publications/emerginggloballabormarket/

Milner, H. V.: *Resisting protectionism: Global industries and the politics of international trade* (Princeton, New Jersey, Princeton University Press, 1988).

Nolan, P. H.: "China at the crossroads", in *Journal of Chinese Economic and Business Studies*, 2005, Vol. 3, No. 1, pp. 1-22.

Nordas, H. K.: *The global textile and clothing industry post the agreement on textiles and clothing* (Geneva, World Trade Organization, 2004).

Palmisano, S.: "The globally integrated enterprise", in *Foreign Affairs*, 2006, Vol. 85, No. 3, pp. 127-136.

Pang, C.: "Chain reaction", in *Textile World Asia*, 2004, Summer.

Pink, D. H.: "The new face of the silicon age: How India became the capital of the computing revolution", in *Wired Magazine*, 2004, Vol. 12, No.2, pp. 1-4.

Polanyi, K.: *The great transformation* (Boston, Massachusetts, Beacon Press, 1944).

Polaski, S.: *Central America and the US face challenge – and chance for historic breakthrough – on workers' rights*, Issue Brief (Washington, DC, Carnegie Endowment for International Peace, Feb. 2003).

—: *Job anxiety is real – and it's global*, Policy Brief No. 30 (Washington, DC, Carnegie Endowment for International Peace, May 2004).

Rai, S.: "Indian services giant hits $1 billion in annual sales", in *New York Times*, 14 Apr. 2004.

Ritzer, G.: *The McDonaldization of society* (Thousand Oaks, California, Pine Forge Press, 2000).

Roach, S.: *Outsourcing, protectionism, and the global labor arbitrage*, Morgan Stanley, Special Economic Study, 11 Nov. 2003.

Rocks, D.; Moon, I.: "Samsung design", in *Business Week Online*, 29 Nov. 2004. http://www.businessweek.com/magazine/content/04_48/b3910003.htm

Rodrik, D.: *Has globalization gone too far?* (Washington, DC, Institute for International Economics, 1997).

—: *The new global economy and developing countries: Making openness work* (Washington, DC, Overseas Development Council, 1999).

—: *What's so special about China's exports?*, Harvard University document, Jan. 2006a.

—: "Goodbye Washington consensus, hello Washington confusion?", Paper prepared for *Journal of Economic Literature*, 2006b, Jan., 29 pp. http://ksghome.harvard.edu/~drodrik/Lessons%20of%20the%201990s20review%20_JEL_pdf

Ruggie, J. G.: "International regimes, transactions and change: Embedded liberalism in the postwar economic order", in *International Organization*, 1982, Vol. 36.

—: *Taking embedded liberalism global: The corporate connection*, Paper presented at the 98th annual meeting of the American Political Science Association, Boston, Massachusetts, 26 Aug.-1 Sep. 2002a.

—: "The new world of corporate responsibility", in *Financial Times*, 25 Oct. 2002b.

Sabel, C.: *Developing economies as Toyota production systems: Why the analogy makes sense, how it can inform industrial policy*, Paper presented at the 2nd annual meeting of the Latin America/Caribbean and Asia/Pacific

Economics and Business Association, 28-29 Nov. 2005, Buenos Aires, Argentina.

Schumer, C.; Roberts, P.C.: "Second thoughts on free trade", in *New York Times*, 6 Jan. 2004, p. 23A.

Schwartz, N. D.: "Down and out in white-collar America", in *Fortune*, 9 June 2003.

Seidman, G.: "Monitoring multinationals: Lessons from the anti-apartheid movement", in *Politics and Society*, 2003, Vol. 31, No. 3, pp. 381-406.

Shenkar, O.: *The Chinese century* (Upper Saddle River, New Jersey, Wharton School Publishing, 2005).

Sonobe, T.; Hu, D.; Otsuka, K.: "Process of cluster formation in China: A case study of a garment town", in *Journal of Development Studies*, 2002, Vol. 39, No. 1, pp. 118-139.

Sturgeon, T.: "How do we define value chains and production networks?", in *IDS Bulletin*, 2001, Vol. 32, No. 3, pp. 9-18.

—; Lee, J.-R.: "Industry co-evolution: A comparison of Taiwan and North American electronics contract manufacturers", in Berger, S.; Lester, R. K. (eds.): *Global Taiwan: Building competitive strengths in a new international economy* (Armonk, New York, Sharpe, 2005), pp. 33-75.

—; Lester, R.: "The new global supply-base: New challenges for local suppliers in East Asia", in Yusuf, S. et al. (eds): *Global production networking and technological change in East Asia* (New York, Oxford University Press, 2004).

United Nations Conference on Trade and Development: *TNCs and the removal of textiles and clothing quotas* (New York and Geneva, UNCTAD, 2005).

United States International Trade Commission: *Shifts in US merchandise trade 2001*, Appendix C (Washington, DC, USITC, 2002).

—: *Textiles and apparel: Assessment of the competitiveness of certain foreign suppliers to the US market*, USITC Publication 3671 (Washington, DC, USITC, 2004).

Waldman, A.: "India takes economic spotlight, and critics are unkind", in *New York Times*, 7 Mar. 2004. http://www.nytimes.com

Wang, J.; Tong, X.: "Clustering in China: Alternative pathways towards global-local linkages", in Gu, S. (ed.): *Technological innovation in China* (Maastricht, The Netherlands, United Nations University, Institute for New Technology, 2002).

Wang, J.; Zhu, H.; Tong, X.: "Industrial districts in a transitional economy: The case of Datang sock and stocking industry in Zhejiang, China", in Lagendijk, A.; Oinas, P.: *Proximity, distance and diversity: Issues on economic interaction and local development* (Burlington, Vermont, Ashgate, 2005), pp. 47-69.

Wang, M. Y.; Meng, X.: "Global-local initiatives in FDI: The experience of Shenzhen, China", in *Asia Pacific Viewpoint*, 2004, Vol. 45, No. 2, pp.181-196.

Williams, O. F. (ed.): *Global codes of conduct: An idea whose time has come* (Notre Dame, Indiana, University of Notre Dame Press, 2000).

Wonacott, P.: "Behind China's export boom, heated battle among factories", in *Wall Street Journal*, 13 Nov. 2003.

Woods, N.: "Global governance and the role of institutions", in Held, D.; McGrew, A. (eds.): *Governing globalization: Power, authority and global governance* (Cambridge, UK, Polity Press, 2002), pp. 25-45.

Zeng, D. Z.: *China's employment challenges and strategies after the WTO accession*, World Bank Policy Research Working Paper 3522, Feb. 2005.

Zhang, Q.; Felmingham, B.: "The role of FDI, exports and spillover effects in the regional development of China", in *Journal of Development Studies*, 2002, Vol. 38, No. 4, pp. 157-178.

Zhang, Z.; To, C.; Cao, N.: "How do industry clusters succeed? A case study in China's textiles and apparel industries", in *Journal of Textile and Apparel Technology and Management*, 2004, Vol. 4, No. 2, pp. 1-10.